Spotlight on Young Children and
Technology

Amy Shillady and Leah Schoenberg Muccio, **Editors**

Derry Koralek, **Chief Publishing Officer**
Edwin C. Malstrom, **Director of Creative Services**
Malini Dominey, **Associate Production Coordinator**
Catherine Cauman, **Associate Editor**
Elizabeth Wegner, **Assistant Editor**

Photo credits: Front cover (*clockwise from top right*): see pp. 47, 9, 6. Back cover (*clockwise from top left*): see pp. 32, 10, 45.

Illustrations: © Gordon Studer

National Association for the Education of Young Children
1313 L Street NW, Suite 500
Washington, DC 20005-4101
202-232-8777 or 800-424-2460
www.naeyc.org

Through its publications program, the National Association for the Education of Young Children (NAEYC) provides a forum for discussion of major issues and ideas in the early childhood field, with the hope of provoking thought and promoting professional growth. The views expressed or implied are not necessarily those of the Association. NAEYC thanks the contributors to this volume.

ISBN 978-1-928896-86-9
NAEYC #267
Library of Congress Control Number: 2012938167

Several of the selections in this book were published originally in volume 67, issue 3, of *Young Children*, NAEYC's award-winning journal. They include "Finding the Education in Educational Technology with Early Learners," by Lilla Dale McManis and Susan B. Gunnewig; "Interactive Whiteboards in Early Childhood Mathematics: Strategies for Effective Implementation in Pre-K–Grade 3," by Sandra M. Linder; "Touch Tablet Surprises: A Preschool Teacher's Story," by Rena Shifflet, Cheri Toledo, and Cassandra Mattoon; "Exploring Elephant Seals in New Jersey: Preschoolers Use Collaborative Multimedia Albums," by Victoria B. Fantozzi; and "iDocument: How Smartphones and Tablets Are Changing Documentation in Preschool and Primary Classrooms," by Will Parnell and Jackie Bartlett. "Young Children and Computers: Storytelling and Learning in a Digital Age," by Bonnie Blagojevic, Suzanne Chevalier, Anneke MacIsaac, Linda Marie Hitchcock, and Bobbi Frechette, first appeared in *Teaching Young Children*, volume 3, issue 5.

"Technology and Interactive Media as Tools in Early Childhood Programs Serving Children from Birth through Age 8," a joint position statement of NAEYC and the Fred Rogers Center for Early Learning and Children's Media at Saint Vincent College, was adopted in January 2012 and is available online at www.naeyc.org/files/naeyc/file/positions/PS_technology_WEB2.pdf.

Contents

On the opening page of several articles, NAEYC's logo and the numbers indicate which of the 10 NAEYC Early Childhood Program Standards those articles address—information for early childhood programs for young children seeking NAEYC Accreditation or improving program quality.

 2,3

Spotlight on **Young Children** and
Technology

© Gordon Studer

A few years ago while teaching kindergarten, I was using a disposable camera to document the children's learning. After Cameron and Sabir made a particularly intricate pattern using lacing beads, I quickly snapped a photo. Right after the click Sabir asked, "Can I see the picture?" Sabir was very surprised when I told him my camera didn't show a picture right away and that we would have to wait to see it. He was so familiar with digital cameras that he'd never experienced the "old-fashioned" technology I was using!

Right in that moment, the meaning of the term **digital native** ("people who have grown up in social conditions where digital technology has been an integral part of their lives" [Zevenbergen & Logan 2008, 37]) became crystal clear to me. The children in my classroom, and young children across the country, are most definitely digital natives. But what does that mean for me and other teachers and for the children and their families? I started to think more about the implications for teaching young children in a digital age. With technology so fundamentally woven into the lives of children, how can I use cutchildren's learning and growth? How can I at the same time build children's digital literacy and digital citizenship? What about issues of equity and access?

Children are naturally drawn to technology, and there is an unquestionable role for technology in the early childhood classroom. But my questions from the classroom still resonate as we consider how to effectively and appropriately integrate technology into early childhood settings. The articles in this book offer answers, and are shaped around the new joint position statement on young children and technology from NAEYC and the Fred Rogers Center for Early Learning and Children's Media at Saint Vincent College "Technology and Interactive Media as Tools in Early Childhood Programs Serving Children from Birth through Age 8." The articles offer examples of ways teachers can use technology to provide appropriate and meaningful learning experiences for young children.

In "Finding the Education in Educational Technology with Early Learners," by **Lilla Dale McManis and Susan B. Gunnewig,** the authors describe the role that technology plays in early childhood education, including recent research about its use in the classroom. The article explains how teachers can evaluate technology to ensure it supports learning goals for children, use it to scaffold children's learning, and integrate it into the curriculum in appropriate and meaningful ways.

In "Preschool Children and Computers: Storytelling and Learning in a Digital Age" by **Bonnie Blagojevic, Suzanne Chevalier, Anneke MacIsaac, Linda Marie Hitchcock, and Bobbi Frechette,** the authors provide tips and resources for teachers to intentionally plan engaging ways children can use computers. Teachers tap into children's interest in computers as a tool to promote additional learning opportunities through digital storytelling for all children, including children who are dual language learners, and to promote family involvement.

Sandra M. Linder's "Interactive Whiteboards in Early Childhood Mathematics: Strategies for Effective Implementation in Pre-K–Grade 3" describes strategies for using technology—particularly interactive whiteboards (IWBs)—to teach young children math skills. Children use IWBs, virtual manipulatives, and other technology to represent data, analyze patterns, and explore parallel and intersecting lines in their surrounding environment.

"Touch Tablet Surprises: A Preschool Teacher's Story," by **Rena Shifflet, Cheri Toledo, and Cassandra Mattoon,** shares one teacher's experiences introducing touch tablets in a preschool classroom. Children eagerly explore the new technology and work together to create illustrations using a drawing application. The teacher reflects her amazement at the ease with which children use the technology and their ability to appreciate and distinguish between real-life and virtual experiences.

Philippa H. Campbell and M. Jeanne Wilcox's "Using Assistive Technology to Promote Inclusion in Early Childhood Settings" introduces the definition, purposes, and examples of assistive technology (AT). The authors describe how teachers can help children with special needs use AT devices to increase, maintain, and improve their growing skills. Teachers of young children with a range of individual needs use AT to help children join in all activities in order to be fully included as members of their classroom community.

Victoria B. Fantozzi's "Exploring Elephant Seals in New Jersey: Preschoolers Use Collaborative Multimedia Albums" shares how teachers can use VoiceThread and other web-based technology. Teachers create presentations using video clips, voice recordings, and images while traveling to different parts of the United States and Mexico. Children engage with the teachers and others by submitting their questions and responding to the images, extending their learning beyond the walls of the classroom.

The authors of "iDocument: How Smartphones and Tablets Are Changing Documentation in Preschool and Primary Classrooms"—**Will Parnell and Jackie Bartlett**—share their experiences and strategies using mobile technology to document young children's learning. One teacher makes audio and video recordings of children, which she plays back to them, helping them extend their thinking. The other uses a smartphone to photograph children's explorations of cat faces, which are posted to the classroom blog, allowing families to join their children's learning experiences.

The book ends with the joint position statement. The statement offers guidance—based on research about how young children learn and develop—on both the opportunities and the challenges of using technology and interactive media in early childhood settings.

I hope these ideas inspire you to use technology in new, exciting ways.

—*Leah Schoenberg Muccio, Co-Editor*

Reference

Zevenbergen, R., & H. Logan. 2008. "Computer Use by Preschool Children: Rethinking Practice as Digital Natives Come to Preschool." *Australian Journal of Early Childhood* 33 (1): 37–44. www.earlychildhoodaustralia.org.au/australian_journal_of_early_childhood/ajec_index_abstracts/computer_use_by_preschool_children.html.

Finding the Education in Educational Technology with Early Learners

Lilla Dale McManis and Susan B. Gunnewig

© Gordon Studer

Lilla Dale McManis, PhD, is research director for Hatch Early Childhood in Winston-Salem, North Carolina, where she conducts research in education technology for early learners. Previously a teacher and teacher educator, she now focuses on understanding learning environments and positive outcomes for young children.

Susan B. Gunnewig, MEd, develops content for technological hardware and platforms at Hatch Early Childhood. Previously on the faculty of the Children's Learning Institute at the University of Texas Medical School, Susan cocreated the Texas School Readiness project, participated in a number of federal grants, and has been a teacher and administrator.

naeyc ® 2, 3

> "Computers have things on them, and when you go there, they have the things you're on."
> — *Owen*, Age 4

Ms. Robin is ready to begin the day. She has reviewed today's goals with Ms. Jan, the teaching assistant, prepared activities for the interactive whiteboard (a large computer-driven touchscreen mounted on the classroom wall), tested the desktop computer software, and charged her digital camera and tablet. We'll catch up with Ms. Robin later to see how the day unfolds.

As many educators and parents have observed, today's children are exposed to advanced technology at an early age, with tablets, e-readers, and smartphones being some prevalent choices (Gutnik et al. 2011; Rideout 2011). Experiences with technology can pave the way for unprecedented learning opportunities. However, without an education component, technology cannot reach its full potential for supporting children's learning and development. In early childhood programs, the education component often means adults being nearby, interacting with children and providing opportunities for peer-to-peer learning to encourage children to gain the skills they need for succeeding in school.

While the literature establishes the use of educational technology and positive outcomes for children (see reviews by Glaubke 2007; McCarrick & Li 2007; Penuel et al. 2009), it also indicates that technology needs to (1) be developmentally appropriate for children, (2) include tools to help teachers implement the technology successfully, and (3) be integrated into the classroom and curriculum (see Clements & Sarama 2003; Glaubke 2007; NAEYC & Fred Rogers Center 2012). In this article, we will discuss these criteria and provide a practical plan, examples, and a tool for evaluating, using, and integrating educational technology in early childhood programs.

Setting the stage

Teachers have been using technology of one type or another with children for decades, but the development of new technologies and their presence in classrooms is increasing rapidly. Interactive single-touch—and now multitouch—screens in a variety of sizes, from interactive whiteboards to tablets, have changed the way children engage with technology. Alongside these is the explosion in learning content, particularly for mobile devices.

Whether traditional or newer, educational technology plays an important role in children's learning when it is based on research, child development theory, and developmentally appropriate practices, and when it aligns with curriculum goals.

The potential for early childhood education

Research shows that computer use supports and increases young children's skills in the social, cognitive, language, literacy, writing, and mathematics realms. Children in early childhood classrooms interact with peers when using computers. They share and help one another, ask for and provide information and explanations, and

© Ellen B. Senisi

Adult guidance for children using computers is associated with increases in abstract reasoning, planning behavior, visual-motor coordination, and visual memory.

collaborate to solve problems (Heft & Swaminathan 2002; Wang & Ching 2003). Adult guidance for children using computers is associated with increases in abstract reasoning, planning behavior, visual-motor coordination, and visual memory (Primavera, Wiederlight, & DiGiacomo 2001; Nir-Gal & Klein 2004). For example, teachers can help children focus on tasks by telling them to look carefully at an action on the screen and observe what is happening, or by asking them what they need to do in a particular situation presented while using a software program.

When teachers support children and media-rich content is integrated with the curriculum, technology experiences are associated with better language and literacy outcomes, such as letter recognition, sequencing, and sounds; listening and comprehension; vocabulary; and understanding concepts about stories and print (Primavera, Wiederlight, & DiGiacomo 2001; Nir-Gal & Klein 2004; Penuel et al. 2009). For instance, children who had daily access to a large library of educational software and teacher supervision made gains, but those with a weekly session with a mentor who facilitated use of the technology made even greater gains (Primavera, Wiederlight, & DiGiacomo 2001). When children use computers with adult support, their math concepts increase for number recognition, counting, shape recognition and composition, and sorting (Primavera, Wiederlight, & DiGiacomo 2001; Clements & Sarama 2007).

The research on newer technologies and applications has yet to catch up with their availability to children, but there are promising indications. Researchers observe greater collaboration among preschoolers when they use interactive whiteboards (IWBs) than when they use traditional desktop computers (nontouch screen, with mouse and keyboard)

© Bonnie Blagojevic

lary and phonological awareness, with children ages 3 to 5 making the most gains (Chiong & Shuler 2010). A recent study of kindergartners randomly assigned to use an iPad to focus on literacy found that the children using the tablet had consistently greater gains than those not using tablets. The researchers found notably strong effects for the iPad children's level of phonemic awareness and ability to represent sounds with letters (Bebell, Dorris, & Muir 2012).

Less access and use seen with preschool teachers

According to two studies sponsored by PBS (Public Broadcasting Service & Grunwald Associates 2009; 2011), K–12 teachers seem to embrace technology and digital resources, but preschool teachers use such technology and digital resources less often. With regard to the devices themselves, and the Internet in particular, the studies report that preschool teachers have less access.

A recent study with early childhood teachers and providers, conducted by the Fred Rogers Center for Early Learning and Children's Media, supports this finding. Only a little more than half of the teachers say their classrooms have computers (Wartella et al. 2010). Half of the teachers surveyed by PBS felt that the content in fee-based technology resources, such as games or activities from videos or the Internet, is not appropriate for the ages and abilities of the children they teach. This may affect teachers' ability to integrate technology as well. While both K–12 and preschool teachers agree that digital media and resources are more effective when integrated into the curriculum, preschool teachers are more likely to use these resources in very limited ways. For example, preschool teachers reported that they limited their use of technology mostly to downloading images and using digital cameras (PBS & Grunwald Associates 2011).

(Wood 2001). McManis, Gunnewig, and McManis (2010) found gains in preschoolers' literacy and math skills in classrooms using an IWB preloaded with school-readiness activities. Usability studies with the newest technologies, particularly mobile ones such as tablets, find that preschool children learn to use the devices quickly, independently, and confidently and explore freely (Couse & Chen 2010; Michael Cohen Group & USDOE 2011). Findings related to outcomes for learning from educational content on mobile devices are beginning to come in. A study with iPod touch devices and PBS-created content for children ages 3 to 7 found that the children made gains in vocabu-

For technology to be developmentally appropriate, it should be responsive to the ages and developmental levels of the children, to their individual needs and interests, and to their social and cultural contexts.

Is the technology developmentally appropriate?

Research is under way, but we still must find strategies now to ensure that new technologies are educationally sound. The 2012 joint position statement on technology and interactive media use with young children, from NAEYC and the Fred Rogers Center, offers several important insights. It affirms that for technology to be developmentally appropriate, it should be responsive to the ages and developmental levels of the children, to their individual needs and interests, and to their social and cultural contexts.

One of the most critical needs identified is support for early childhood practitioners in gaining the knowledge and skills to select and use technology in appropriate ways with young children. Acknowledging that there can be a negative impact on learning and development when educators lack the needed knowledge and skills to do so, the importance of providing resources, guidance, and support for teachers becomes even more pressing (NAEYC & Fred Rogers Center 2012).

Doing some groundwork before considering options will help ensure that you determine the best educational technology for children. A first step is to establish learning goals for the children. The goals might include fostering children's literacy and math or social-emotional development. Some products promise successful attention to and integration of all areas of learning, but it is not likely they can deliver and still meet instructional excellence. We recommend ranking and prioritizing the learning goals, although technology does not have to be used to meet all goals.

Next is identifying the hardware on hand or that you'd like for your classroom, because the hardware drives the children's experiences and the available choices for software. For example, software designed as applications (apps) on tablets does not generally transfer to interactive whiteboards.

Now it's time to consider the content of software programs. We will first look at an evaluation tool and then focus on five areas of software programs that have the potential to strongly impact children's learning experiences: the educational value of a program, its ability to engage a child in learning, its child-friendliness, the interactivity between child and program, and a software program's ability to monitor a child's progress. These areas are informed by considerations from researchers and policy makers (for example, Clements & Sarama 2003; Glaubke 2007; International Society for Technology in Education 2008; Penuel et al. 2009). This list is not exhaustive, and some considerations, such as durability and cost of the technology, are not presented here because they do not focus directly on educational aspects.

Key Steps to Successfully Evaluating Educational Technology

1. Establish learning goals for the children.
2. Identify the hardware or device(s) you have or would like to have.
3. Analyze features and content of the software/program in meeting learning goals.
4. Plan how the educational technology will be integrated into the curriculum.

Analyzing software content: An evaluation tool

Hatch Early Learning created *The Early Childhood Educational Technology Evaluation Toolkit* (McManis & Parks 2011) as the result of a review of the literature on elements to consider when evaluating educational technology for early learners.

The toolkit addresses aspects of current practices and capabilities that newer technologies can support, such as progress-monitoring features. Additionally, it focuses on the context in which the educational technology will be used, such as the ages of the children, type of learners (for example, children who have special needs or children who are dual language learners), type of device (more traditional along with newer technologies), and factors that affect integration, such as professional development to support teachers' technology skills. The toolkit includes a worksheet and accompanying explanations and examples. It can be accessed at www.hatchearlychildhood.com/toolkit.

While individual teachers can use the toolkit, one intent of its use is to bring together a team of invested parties in an early childhood education program. This could be any combination of members—teachers, administrators, parents, technology coaches, curriculum directors, IT personnel, and so on—that makes sense and works for your program. They can use the toolkit to evaluate existing educational technology and for future selections. The toolkit is a support for gathering information in a systematic and thoughtful manner to facilitate dialogue about options. It can also help families better understand a teacher's or program's decisions and contribute to families' own efforts to evaluate technology for their children. For example, if a program decides to invest in a software package and has evaluated this choice with the toolkit, staff can share the ratings with families to help them understand why that particular software was chosen as part of the curriculum offered to their children.

Early Childhood Educational Technology Evaluation Toolkit

Complete the following worksheet for each major educational technology purchase consideration. Please see accompanying directions for further explanation and examples.

Date: _____ Evaluator(s): _____

Organization: _____

Age group: _____ Older Toddlers _____ Preschoolers _____ School Age (Grades _____)

Type: ____ Regular Education ____ Special Needs (Disability: _____) ____ ELL ____ Title 1

GOALS	
	_____ a. Approaches to learning (curiosity, attention, flexible thinking/creativity, persistence)
	_____ b. Language/Literacy _____ c. Mathematics _____ d. Science
	_____ e. Social Studies _____ f. Social-Emotional (cooperation, collaboration, identifying emotions)

HARDWARE	
	_____ a. Desktop or laptop computer (mouse and keyboard) _____ b. Desktop or laptop computer (touch screen)
	_____ c. Interactive whiteboard _____ d. Tablet _____ e. Multi-touch table or surface

SOFTWARE

Software Title: _____ (1 = No 2 = Unsure 3 = Somewhat 4 = Yes)

Category	Item	1	2	3	4
1. Educational	a. Learning versus focus on winning?	1	2	3	4
	b. Content research and/or learning standards based?	1	2	3	4
	c. Feedback informative/teaches?	1	2	3	4
2. Appropriate	a. Appropriate cognitive skill(s)/subject matter?	1	2	3	4
	b. Set in interesting/appealing context?	1	2	3	4
	c. Pre/non-readers can navigate?	1	2	3	4
	d. Free from bias?	1	2	3	4
3. Child-Friendly	a. Simple/clear choices?	1	2	3	4
	b. Multiple, positive opportunities for success?	1	2	3	4
	c. After adult support, children can use independently?	1	2	3	4
4. Enjoyable/Engaging	a. Enough activities with variety?	1	2	3	4
	b. Appropriate use of rewards?	1	2	3	4
	c. Realistic graphics and appealing to intended age?	1	2	3	4
	d. Activities match well to attention span?	1	2	3	4
5. Progress Monitoring/Assessment	a. Covers all the key areas the software teaches?	1	2	3	4
	b. Easy to use and interpret?	1	2	3	4
6. Individualizing Features	a. Can be customized for child's needs?	1	2	3	4
	b. Allows creation of new activities?	1	2	3	4

INTEGRATION					
	a. Initial training/professional development on integration included?	1	2	3	4
	b. Ongoing training/professional development opportunities?	1	2	3	4

SCORE		
	(Total Score ÷ 80) × 100 = _____ (90-100 = A, 80-89 = B, 70-79 = C, 60-69 = D, <59 = F)	_____ Purchase _____ Continue to Consider this Option _____ Do Not Purchase _____ Consider other Options

COMMENTS	

Educational value

Is the content based on research/standards? The skills the software helps promote should be those deemed necessary by research and/or applicable early learning guidelines. For example, the content aligns with recommendations by the National Research Council (2009) for mathematics, or the content aligns with the early learning standards used in your state or program.

Does the software follow the correct developmental course and effective teaching paths? The content should follow and use the appropriate teaching path before asking children to make responses. For instance, the software introduces letter names before asking children to identify letters, and children learn about individual geometric shapes before using them to make patterns.

© Ellen B. Senisi

Engagement to enhance learning

Are the activities presented in a playlike fashion? Qualities of play should be obvious, including offering children opportunities to make choices and create scenarios and encouraging children to use their imaginations. Presentation in the context of a game can be appropriate, but not when the object is winning over learning.

Are rewards used appropriately? Teachers should make the association for children between the internal reward, such as feeling satisfaction in helping a peer or mastering a skill, and the external reward, such as collecting a star or points. Feedback such as "You helped your friend feel better" or "You kept at it and figured that out!" helps children want to engage with the activities for the positive internal feelings.

Child-friendly

Are there multiple opportunities for success? Children should be able to re-process (think again about the situation and information and apply a more effective strategy) and respond again. Equally important is whether a program is intuitive enough to determine when a child is repeatedly not experiencing success. Does it include a mechanism to help the child, such as making a tutorial available, moving the child back a level, and/or informing the teacher that additional instruction is needed?

Can children use the software independently? After adult modeling, children should be able to proceed with minimal assistance. Continually getting stuck or confused isn't conducive to learning, nor does it encourage a positive feeling about using technology. Understandable and logical instructions integrated with supports and prompts are essential. It is also important for children to get help when they need it. Independence should not be taken to mean working alone at all times. Children working with technology in teacher-led activities or in peer groups can be a powerful type of learning, particularly for additional language and social skills development.

Interactivity

Does the program respond to and/or can it be customized to the child? The most meaningful interactions between a child and technology take place when a software program is adapted to suit the child's needs. This occurs when the teacher can set a predetermined level, the program presents the appropriate level or activities, or the teacher can move the child manually through levels as the child is ready. This can be particularly important for children who have special needs, are dual language learners, or have less access to technology.

Does the program allow for creation of new activities? Such options increase usability, interest, and higher-order thinking. This feature can take many forms. Children might use a basic drawing application to create their own representation of pets versus having to always choose from a predetermined set of pictures offered in a software package. A focus in this area can substantially increase children's understanding so that technology is truly a learning tool.

Progress monitoring

This area relates to information teachers gain as a result of children's use of technology.

Is there a progress-monitoring feature? Such a feature collects information about how children are interacting with the learning content (often as automatic capturing of the responses children make compared to a set criterion) and then shows how children are moving toward competency. For example, depending on the criteria design, children may show mastery as a percent (100% mastery, 80% mastery, 60% mastery, and so on) of being able to choose the numeral that represents a set of objects they see over a number of opportunities to do so (they choose the numeral *5* for five bears having a picnic). This feature is more in demand because of the

Children working with technology in teacher-led activities or in peer groups can be a powerful type of learning, particularly for additional language and social skills development.

growing recognition of the critical role monitoring progress plays in guiding instruction to reach positive child outcomes (Shapiro 2008).

How are the results presented, and are they easily used? Some programs provide reports at levels such as the class, group, and/or individual child. Reports that provide more specific information and give that information over time are most useful—for example, breaking out the skills that make up phonological awareness versus one global indicator, or showing children's progress monthly or quarterly versus just at the end of the use of the software program.

Another example of presenting results of children's learning is through digital portfolios. Digital portfolios serve the same purpose as traditional portfolios—to be an authentic record of a child's learning process. The main difference is that the items in the portfolio are in a digital (electronic) format versus the usual paper format. Some, but not all, technology and accompanying software have a digital portfolio function so the work children complete/create on the computer can be stored this way. For example, certain interactive whiteboards have a recorder that, when enabled, captures the actual movements the child is making as she interacts with the

content on the board and records her verbalizations. Teachers can retrieve and play the video to analyze the child's processes as often as they like. For instance, if a child is repeatedly having difficulty forming certain letters, the teacher can see very clearly exactly where in a letter's formation the child is struggling.

Additionally, showing families their child actually creating and speaking about what he is doing is a powerful experience. It allows teachers to both showcase a child's work and discuss with families exemplary learning as well as areas where the child may not be meeting a learning goal.

The role of supported learning in using technology: Scaffolding

When children use technology, teachers often think about demonstrating, trouble-shooting, or monitoring turn taking. They tend to give less attention to interacting with children to bolster positive learning approaches and increase children's knowledge. However, doing so exemplifies the education in educational technology. Putting this into practice with technology means active engagement, group participation, interactivity and feedback, and connecting technology to real-world contexts. One approach is scaffolding children's use of technology.

When teachers do so, children can meet established learning goals more often, work more effectively, and use higher levels of thinking than when they are expected to solve tasks without assistance (Barbuto et al. 2003; Yelland & Masters 2007). Yelland and Masters identify three types of scaffolding teachers can implement when using technology with children: cognitive, technical, and affective.

Cognitive scaffolding

Teachers use *cognitive scaffolding* to develop children's understanding of concepts, and it most obviously resembles traditional scaffolding between adult/teacher and child. Activities include questioning, modeling, and encouraging collaboration with peers. Keeping in mind the power of play in learning, these scaffolds can make use of spontaneity, choice, creativity, and imagination. One method is to use an app for mobile devices that allows children to create animated stories. Working individually or with peers, children can create, dictate, and/or illustrate a story on a tablet. They can retrieve the story later and continue working on it while the teacher encourages (scaffolds) use of new vocabulary and more complete story structure. For example, the children may begin by learning simple words about a farm animal, such as *chicken,* and over time learn *hen, rooster,* and *chicks.* They bring this vocabulary to life by finding or drawing

pictures that represent additional words and placing these in the story.

Technical scaffolding

Technical scaffolding uses the features of the technology to support learning. That is, the technology itself can facilitate understanding and problem solving. For example, computer programs are easily able to move shapes around in space, so an activity that helps children understand that a shape stays constant, no matter its orientation, uses technical scaffolding. Another example is a computer program that moves the activity's level up or down, based on a child's responses, so that the child works or plays at a level appropriate for her.

Affective scaffolding

Yelland and Masters also identify children's need for *affective scaffolding* to help keep them on task and encourage higher levels of thinking when using technology. Examples are a teacher staying physically close by when a child uses a computer program and giving a thumbs-up when the child is successful, or if the child experiences difficulty, saying, "I saw you do that yesterday; try to remember how you did it" and "I thought you could figure that out!"

The software program itself can offer affective scaffolding through positive feedback, often seen with characters accompanying a child on her journey. For example, a character may show the child what to do or may appear after a portion of the game or activity to affirm or encourage the child to keep going.

Integration

There is growing recognition of the importance of incorporating technology in meaningful and authentic ways into the curriculum and day-to-day practices, and of the teacher's crucial role in the full development and use of technology in the early childhood classroom (Swan et al. 2002; ISTE 2008; USDOE 2010; NAEYC & Fred Rogers Center 2012). The joint position statement from NAEYC and the Fred Rogers Center emphasizes this eloquently: "The adult's role is critical in making certain that thoughtful planning, careful implementation, reflection, and evaluation all guide decision making about how to introduce and integrate any form of technology or media into the classroom experience" (6). However, research also documents that technology integration does not happen to the degree it needs to in order to fully realize its potential to support children's learning (Swan et al. 2002; ISTE 2008; USDOE 2010; Barron et al. 2011; NAEYC & Fred

Rogers Center 2012).

The lack of time for professional development is one of the most serious obstacles to fully integrating technology into the curriculum that teachers identify (USDOE 2010). Feasible options for early childhood programs to consider include built-in technology supports and learning communities.

Built-in supports

When considering a software program, look for features that (a) support teachers in a technical sense, such as tutorials and help functions; (b) guide the use of the content, such as sample lessons, extension activities, and options for teachers to create their own additional activities; and (c) bolster teachers' ability to effectively provide instructional support to children, such as results and reports from the progress-monitoring features in software programs and explicit connections to the curriculum or to learning standards.

Learning communities

Learning communities represent a powerful approach for bringing people together around a common goal. There is no one-size-fits-all when it comes to forming and participating in a learning community. There are, however, several characteristics of effective learning communities, such as those identified by Ellen Galinsky (2012). Among others, these include bringing new players together, members learning from and with one another rather than always from an "expert," and an active focus on learning.

A recent report from the Joan Ganz Cooney Center, "Take a Giant Step: A Blueprint for Teaching Children in a Digital Age" (Barron et al. 2011), lays out national goals and immediate actions, acknowledging that leaders in education must restructure time and staffing so that teachers can work together and with students to use technology. The report includes recommendations for creating communities of practice that have abundant collaboration among teachers and for training early educators in integrating technology using developmentally appropriate practices.

Teachers gathering regularly in small groups to discuss their own goals, and methods for meeting them, is probably the easiest way to start a learning community. A second is curriculum development teams consisting of staff gathering to develop lessons using technology. A third kind of learning community includes technology coaches and mentors, as research shows novice teachers make good progress alongside skilled partners (Chen & Chang 2006).

Visiting Ms. Robin's preschool class for a technology-infused morning

This week's theme in Ms. Robin's class is "The Ants Go Marching." The children learn about living and nonliving things, related vocabulary, being part of a group, phonological awareness, and counting. On arrival, children write their names on the interactive whiteboard using their choice of the pens, their fingers, or a tennis ball. At circle time Ms. Robin plays "The Ants Go Marching" song, inviting children to march to the carpet. She uses the IWB to focus on the concepts living and nonliving, introducing vocabulary and having children move objects while encouraging each child to talk and share ideas. She finishes with a read-aloud on the topic.

Next, they take a walk outside. Ms. Robin takes digital pictures as the children point out living and nonliving things. Then the children play on the playground equipment, with Ms. Robin encouraging them to imagine they are ants or bees working together to look for food. Now it is time to go to centers—dramatic play, blocks, writing, art, and computer.

Ms. Jan, the teaching assistant, visits the computer center where a child is engaged in phonological awareness activities. She encourages him to say the sounds aloud. Others work with Ms. Robin on the IWB to practice counting. She has pulled up a picture of an ant and used the replicator (a feature that makes duplicates or copies) to make graphic manipulatives. The children use their fingers to touch and move the ants as they count.

While the children nap, Ms. Robin downloads the pictures from the walk onto her tablet. She will use photo management software to enlarge or crop the pictures, adjust brightness/contrast, and rotate/flip, as needed. She collaborates with the children to choose a set of the photos to create a class book about living and nonliving things. The children will take turns bringing

There is growing recognition of the importance of incorporating technology in meaningful and authentic ways into the curriculum and day-to-day practices, and of the teacher's crucial role in the full development and use of technology in the early childhood classroom.

home the book and a DVD (a video Ms. Robin will make of Ms. Jan turning the pages slowly) for families and children to read and view together. Ms. Robin is looking forward to beginning this project tomorrow!

Summary

Finding the education in educational technology is important for supporting early learners' positive development. We have discussed educational technology in three areas: developmental appropriateness, supported implementation, and classroom and curriculum integration. When considered together, these areas can strengthen the potential of technology to facilitate meaningful learning for young children. We hope the ideas, examples, and evaluation toolkit support your own technology journey with the children in your program.

References

Barbuto, L.M., S. Swaminathan, J. Trawick-Smith, & J.L. Wright. 2003. "The Role of the Teacher in Scaffolding Children's Interactions in a Technological Environment: How a Technology Project Is Transforming Preschool Teacher Practices in Urban Schools." In *Young Children and Learning Technologies,* eds. J. Wright, A. McDougall, J. Murnane, & H.J. Lowe, 13–20. Conferences in Research and Practice in Information series. Melbourne, Victoria: Australian Computer Society.

Barron, B., G. Cayton-Hodges, L. Bofferding, C. Copple, L. Darling-Hammond, & M. Levine. 2011. "Take a Giant Step: A Blueprint for Teaching Children in a Digital Age." New York: The Joan Ganz Cooney Center at Sesame Workshop. http://joanganzcooneycenter.org/upload_kits/jgcc_takea giantstep.pdf.

Bebell, D., S. Dorris, & M. Muir. 2012. "Emerging Results from the Nation's First Kindergarten Implementation of iPads." Research summary.https://s3.amazonaws.com/hackedu/ Adv2014_ResearchSum120216.pdf.

Chen, J.-Q., & C. Chang. 2006. "Testing the *Whole Teacher* Approach to Professional Development: A Study of Enhancing Early Childhood Teachers' Technology Proficiency." *Early Childhood Research & Practice* 8 (1). http://ecrp.uiuc. edu/v8n1/chen.html.

Chiong, C., & C. Shuler. 2010. "Learning: Is There an App for That? Investigations of Young Children's Usage and Learning with Mobile Devices and Apps." New York: The Joan Ganz Cooney Center at Sesame Workshop. http://pbskids. org/read/files/cooney_learning_apps.pdf.

Clements, D.H., & J. Sarama. 2003. "Strip Mining for Gold: Research and Policy in Educational Technology: A Response to 'Fool's Gold.'" *AACE Journal* 11 (1): 7–69.

Clements, D.H., & J. Sarama. 2007. "Effects of a Preschool Mathematics Curriculum: Summative Research on the Building Blocks Project." *Journal for Research in Mathematics Education* 38 (2): 136–63.

Couse, L.J., & D.W. Chen. 2010. "A Tablet Computer for Young Children? Exploring Its Viability for Early Childhood Education." *Journal of Research on Technology in Education* 43 (1): 75–98.

Galinsky, E. 2012. "Learning Communities: An Emerging Phenomenon." *Young Children* 67 (1): 20–27.

Glaubke, C.R. 2007. "The Effects of Interactive Media on Preschoolers' Learning: A Review of the Research and Recommendations for the Future." Oakland, CA: Children Now. www.childrennow.org/uploads/documents/prek_interac tive_learning_2007.pdf.

Gutnick, A.L., M. Robb, L. Takeuchi, & J. Kotler. 2011. "Always Connected: The New Digital Media Habits of Young Children." New York: The Joan Ganz Cooney Center at Sesame Workshop. www.ictliteracy.info/rf.pdf/jgcc_alwaysconnec ted.pdf.

Heft, T.M., & S. Swaminathan. 2002. "The Effects of Computers on the Social Behavior of Preschoolers." *Journal of Research in Childhood Education* 16 (2): 162–74.

International Society for Technology in Education. 2008. "National Educational Technology Standards for Teachers." Washington, DC: Author. www.iste.org/standards/ nets-for-teachers/nets-for-teachers-2008.aspx.

McCarrick, K., & X. Li. 2007. "Buried Treasure: The Impact of Computer Use on Young Children's Social, Cognitive, Language Development and Motivation." *AACE Journal* 15 (1): 73–95.

McManis, L.D., S.B. Gunnewig, & M.H. McManis. 2010. Exploring the Contribution of a Content-Infused Interactive Whiteboard for School Readiness. Winston-Salem, NC: Hatch Early Childhood. ED528703. www.eric.ed.gov/PDFS/ ED528703.pdf.

McManis, L.D., & J. Parks. 2011. "Evaluating Technology for Early Learners."E-book and toolkit. Winston-Salem, NC: Hatch Early Learning.www.hatchearlychildhood.com/ toolkit.

Michael Cohen Group & USDOE [US Department of Education]. 2011. "Young Children, Apps & iPad." New York: Michael Cohen Group. www.mcgrc.com/wp-content/ uploads/2011/07/ipad-study-cover-page-report-mcg-info_ new-online.pdf.

Teachers gathering regularly in small groups to discuss their own goals, and methods for meeting them, is probably the easiest way to start a learning community.

NAEYC & Fred Rogers Center for Early Learning and Children's Media at Saint Vincent College. 2012. "Technology and Interactive Media as Tools in Early Childhood Programs Serving Children from Birth through Age 8." Joint position statement. Washington, DC: NAEYC. www.naeyc.org/files/naeyc/file/positions/PS_technology_WEB2.pdf.

National Research Council. 2009. *Mathematics Learning in Early Childhood: Paths Toward Excellence and Equity.* Committee on Early Childhood Mathematics, C.T. Cross, T.A. Woods, H. Schweingruber, eds. Center for Education, Division of Behavioral and Social Sciences and Education. Washington, DC: The National Academies Press. www.nap.edu/catalog.php?record_id=12519.

Nir-Gal, O., & P.S. Klein. 2004. "Computers for Cognitive Development in Early Childhood—The Teacher's Role in the Computer Learning Environment." *Information Technology in Childhood Education Annual*, 2004, 97–119.

Penuel, W.R., S. Pasnik, L. Bates, E. Townsend, L.P. Gallagher, C. Llorente, & N. Hupert. 2009. "Preschool Teachers Can Use a Media-Rich Curriculum to Prepare Low-Income Children for School Success: Results of a Randomized Controlled Trial." New York: Education Development Center; Menlo Park, CA: SRI International. www.cct.edc.org/rtl/pdf/RTLEvalReport.pdf.

Primavera, J., P.P. Wiederlight, & T.M. DiGiacomo. 2001. "Technology Access for Low-Income Preschoolers: Bridging the Digital Divide." Paper presented at the American Psychological Association Annual Meeting, in San Francisco. www.knowledgeadventure.com/jumpstartworld/_docs/ChildTechnology_White_Paper.pdf.

Public Broadcasting Service & Grunwald Associates. 2009. "Digitally Inclined: Annual Survey of Educators' Use of Media and Technology." Arlington, VA: Author. www.pbs.org/teachers/_files/pdf/annual-pbs-survey-report.pdf.

Public Broadcasting Service & Grunwald Associates. 2011. "Deepening Connections: Teachers Increasingly Rely on Media and Technology." Arlington, VA: Author. www.pbs.org/teachers/grunwald/pbs-grunwald-2010.pdf.

Rideout, V. 2011. "Zero to Eight: Children's Media Use in America." San Francisco, CA: Common Sense Media. www.commonsensemedia.org/sites/default/files/research/zerotoeightfinal2011.pdf.

Shapiro, E.S. 2008. "Best Practices in Setting Progress Monitoring Goals for Academic Skill Improvement." In *Best Practices in School Psychology V,* eds. A. Thomas & J. Grimes, 141–57. Bethesda, MD: National Association of School Psychologists.

Swan, K., A. Holmes, J.D. Vargas, S. Jennings, E. Meier, & L. Rubenfeld. 2002. "Situated Professional Development and Technology Integration: The Capital Area Technology and Inquiry in Education [CATIE] Mentoring Program." *Journal of Technology and Teacher Education* 10 (2): 169–90.

US Department of Education. 2010. "Transforming American Education: Learning Powered by Technology." Washington, DC: Office of Educational Technology. www.ed.gov/sites/default/files/netp2010.pdf.

Wang, X.C., & C.C. Ching. 2003. "Social Construction of Computer Experience in a First-Grade Classroom: Social Processes and Mediating Artifacts." *Early Education and Development* 14 (3): 335–61.

Wartella, E., R.L. Schomburg, A.R. Lauricella, M. Robb, & R. Flynn. 2010. "Technology in the Lives of Teachers and Classrooms: Survey of Classroom Teachers and Family Child Care Providers." Latrobe, PA: Fred Rogers Center for Early Learning and Children's Media at St. Vincent College. www.fredrogerscenter.org/media/resources/TechInTheLivesofTeachers.pdf.

Wood, C. 2001. "Interactive Whiteboards: A Luxury Too Far?" *Teaching ICT* 1 (2): 52–62.

Yelland, N., & J. Masters. 2007. "Rethinking Scaffolding in the Information Age." *Computers & Education* 48 (3): 362–82.

Finding the Education in Educational Technology with Early Learners

by Lilla Dale McManis and Susan B. Gunnewig

This article explores developmental appropriateness, adult-supported implementation, and classroom and curriculum integration of educational technology in early childhood settings. It explains key steps teachers can follow and tools they can use to evaluate educational technology, along with ways teachers can support children's use of technology through scaffolding to promote meaningful learning and engagement.

Key messages

1. Children's use of technology can substantially support their learning in all developmental domains.
2. To provide educationally sound and developmentally appropriate experiences, it is important for early childhood educators to use research-based criteria to evaluate existing educational technology and to guide their future selections.
3. It is essential for teachers to scaffold children's use of technology while integrating it into the curriculum and children's day-to-day learning experiences.

In your view

1. What are the three most important themes or key ideas in this article? If possible, compare your choices with those of others who have read the article.
2. How is the content of this article related to applicable early learning standards or other curriculum or program requirements?

Reflect and revisit your practice

1. What ideas in this article affirm your practice? What questions does the article raise about your teaching practices? What new approaches might you try?
2. What kinds of supports do you and other teachers need to try out these new ideas?

Let's talk

1. How do you make decisions about the use of technology in your learning environment? Which of the areas in the section "Analyzing Software Content: An Evaluation Tool" (pp. 7–11) do you consider when selecting technology to use with children? Which areas are new to you? How may these new areas impact the way you will evaluate technology in the future?
2. How do you currently use educational technology to support positive experiences and outcomes with young children? How do you determine children's progress toward learning goals as a result of using educational technology?
3. Who has an influence on what and how educational technology is used in your early childhood setting? How are families involved in this process?
4. Why is professional development on best practices for using technology important? In what ways does your setting provide professional development? What more do you need to know?

Steps you can take

1. Develop a lesson plan with goals and one or two simple learning outcomes for children. Focus on one type of scaffolding support for children using technology—cognitive, technical, or affective (as described on page 11).
2. Implement the lesson with a small group of children. Observe the children throughout the lesson, and record your observations afterward. Determine the degree to which children reached the goals and learning objectives.
3. Share with colleagues how you carried out this activity and your reflections on how the techniques did or did not enhance children's learning. Discuss ways you will refine the techniques the next time you use them.

Glossary

Educational technology—software programs or applications, along with the hardware or device (such as a computer, interactive whiteboard, tablet, or multitouch table), that are used to promote children's development and learning.

Technology scaffolding—purposefully supporting children's learning, while they use educational technology, through techniques such as asking, answering, and inviting questions; encouraging positive feelings about technology; and making use of computer/technological capabilities.

Technology integration—using educational technology with children in a way that is seamlessly woven in with curriculum and is a natural and easy part of the learning experience.

To increase your knowledge

Erikson TEC Center: Technology in Early Childhood, Erikson Institute. www.teccenter.erikson.edu.

The Joan Ganz Cooney Center at Sesame Workshop: www.joanganzcooneycenter.org/Reports.html.

McManis, L.D., & J. Parks. 2011. "Evaluating Technology for Early Learners." eBook and Toolkit. Winston-Salem, NC: Hatch Early Learning. www.hatchearlychildhood.com/toolkit.

Yelland, N., & J. Masters. 2007. "Rethinking Scaffolding in the Information Age." Computers & Education 48 (3): 362–82. www.cblt.soton.ac.uk/multimedia/PDFsMM09/Rethinking%20scaffolding%20in%20the%20info%20age.pdf.

Preschool Children and Computers

Storytelling and Learning in a Digital Age

Bonnie Blagojevic, Suzanne Chevalier,
Anneke MacIsaac, Linda Marie Hitchcock,
and Bobbi Frechette

© Gordon Studer

Young children are surrounded by technology at home, in their community, and, increasingly, in early childhood education programs. Preschoolers use computers to create art, make music, tell and record stories, hear their stories read back to them, and play educational games that can connect with off-screen learning and play. Careful planning of computer use lets children explore these new opportunities.

Kumar sits at the computer using the pencil tool in a software program. He creates a digital drawing of a storm, a current topic of study in his preschool classroom. When he is done, Kumar dictates a story to his teacher, Maria, to go along with the drawing. Maria types Kumar's words. Kumar and Maria then look together through a set of printed name cards stored in a small basket at the computer. He finds the one that says *Kumar*, announcing, "Here it is." Then he chooses a color from the software program's color palette, directing the on-screen pencil tool with the computer mouse. Kumar carefully draws the first letter of his name on his digital artwork. He looks at the *K* on the name card. Not happy with the way his *K* looks, Kumar uses the undo button and tries again. This time he likes the result. Maria is thrilled. This is the first time she has seen Kumar interested

---

Bonnie Blagojevic, CAS, is an education consultant at Morningtown Consulting in Orono, Maine, an adjunct faculty member at the University of Maine, and an Apple Distinguished Educator. Her projects explore ways technology can be used to support early learning and professional development.

Suzanne Chevalier, CAS, is a K–1 DLL specialist at Riverton Elementary School in Portland, Maine. As a teacher, consultant, early literacy coach, and professional development coordinator, Sue has helped early childhood educators integrate technology with intentionality.

Anneke MacIsaac, BA, is a site supervisor at Androscoggin Head Start and Childcare in Lewiston, Maine. As a former early literacy specialist, she assisted teaching staff and children in using computers to enrich the Opening the World of Learning curriculum.

Linda Marie Hitchcock, CDA, is a teacher's aid at Opportunity Alliance in Portland, Maine, where she has worked for 25 years accommodating children and families in this Head Start setting.

Bobbi Frechette, CDA, is the owner/artist of RedSun Designs in Lewiston, Maine. She is working on a BA in psychology, with a focus on helping families who have children with developmental challenges.

Photos by Bonnie Blagojevic / © University of Maine Center for Community Inclusion and Disability Studies.

naeyc ® 2, 3

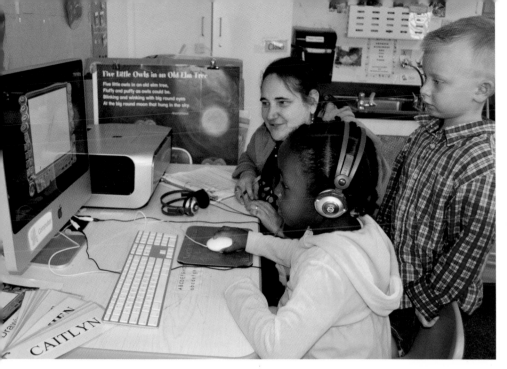

Carly is excited that her story is recognized and shared with her family and friends. She would like to create other stories, and may inspire other children to share their stories.

As children learn to use the computer as a tool for storytelling and skill building, their teachers can encourage them to combine use of this tool with other means of expression. They can help children make connections between computer activities and other learning centers.

Milos and Philip are taking turns creating a "friend" figure using an educational software program. Their preschool teacher, Ana, knows that Milos is new to computer use. She stands nearby, ready to provide support as he learns to move the mouse and clicks to select a body part on the figure. He chooses the feet and decides to make them pointed and green. Using headphones, the boys listen as the descriptive words Milos selects are read aloud. They point to changes Milos is making to the "friend" figure and discuss what is happening. When Milos decides his "friend" is finished, Ana helps him print it. Then it is Philip's turn. When he is finished, the boys each cut out their paper "friends," attach them to cardboard tubes, and bring them to the dramatic play area to use as play figures.

in writing his name despite frequent invitations. Kumar begins to practice his name-writing in other areas, like the writing center. Soon he is writing his name fluently.

Children such as Kumar can build a variety of skills while exploring the functions of a classroom computer. Kumar's teacher thoughtfully considers her goals for children's learning, and the range of computer activities available to the children in her class. She considers children's interests, developmental stages, and abilities when planning appropriate computer activity options for every child.

In the following vignette, Carly, a more experienced computer user, tells a digital story.

Carly, a 4-year-old in Debbie's preschool class, creates a digital "scribble" with many lines and bright colors. Debbie says, "Would you like to tell me about your picture?" Carly answers, "This is a picture of Mommy and Daddy going to the hotel." To better understand Carly's story idea, Debbie asks, "Can you tell me more about what happened? How did they get to the hotel?" She uses the software's audio recording button to record Carly's response: "They're going in a big truck that works there, and they are going to take a bus. And then they are going to go back home and get their medicine and feel better."

Debbie works closely with the children's families, so she realizes that in Carly's story, the hotel is a hospital and the truck is an ambulance. Carly is describing an experience from a year ago that is still important to her. Once finished, Carly can look at her digital drawing and listen to and revisit her recorded story on the computer. Debbie prints two copies of the story. With Carly's permission, she reads the story aloud at circle time, then posts it on the wall where children's work is displayed. Carly takes home the other copy to share with her family.

Integrating computers into the classroom

When first introducing computers to young children, it is best to adopt a "less is more" approach. By starting with only a few programs and activities, teachers and children can become familiar with using them. Teachers can focus on how to use programs in intentional ways to provide the appropriate level of challenge for every learner, and provide support as needed to ensure success. Often

As children learn to use the computer as a tool for storytelling and skill building, their teachers can encourage them to combine use of this tool with other means of expression.

preschool teachers have questions about including computers in their classrooms and using them as effective learning tools. Here are several common questions and the practices we have found useful in our experience.

How and where should I set up the computer center?

• Consider traffic flow, active versus quiet areas, and other logistics when deciding where to locate the center.

• Place the computer strategically to avoid screen glare.

• Include child-size, adjustable furniture (table and chairs), space for two friends (a "doer" and a "viewer"), and headphones to reduce distractions for users and other children.

• Provide reference items such as a picture dictionary, name cards, and an alphabet chart with uppercase and lowercase letters.

• Post a turn-taking sign-up sheet with an attached pencil or marker.

• Designate child-accessible areas to display children's work, such as a low bulletin board to showcase work made using computer technology.

How do I introduce the computer to the children?

• Find out what the children already know about computers and how they work. Ask them, "What do you want to learn to do on the computer?" Note and address their interests.

• Look at and name the parts of a computer, and discuss how it works, with one child or a small group.

• Involve children in developing rules and guidelines for using the computer and printer. Post a list of the rules and guidelines as a reminder.

What strategies are appropriate for teaching children about computers?

• Be clear about your learning goals, and when and why you might use a particular software program.

• Familiarize yourself with the computer *and* with activities in children's software programs before assisting children.

• Introduce and demonstrate aspects of computer use to the whole group. Follow up with support for individuals, as needed. Help children learn basic computer skills, such as how to control the mouse.

• Let children freely explore new software programs (after you have reviewed them).

• Help children become familiar with a particular software activity, like the paint tool options in a drawing program for creating a digital painting and story. Explain the activity during a morning meeting, so children know how to select, do, and exit the activity. Show the computer screen or a printed image of the activity.

• Integrate computer activities with the curriculum to complement educational goals.

Teachers can focus on how to use programs in intentional ways to provide the appropriate level of challenge for every learner, and provide support as needed to ensure success.

• Consider finding extra hands to help. Classroom volunteers might be parents, foster parents, grandparents, other family members, older children, a college student intern, or a teenager doing a community service project.

• Study the classroom schedule to identify when extra hands might be available, and take advantage of opportunities—such as days or times with lower enrollment—to ensure all children have a turn and the support needed to learn to use the computer successfully.

How can computer use support dual language learners?

• Enlist families, staff, and other volunteers to record songs, stories, and frequently used words in English and children's home languages. With a little training, these bilingual volunteers can learn to use the computer to support children in expressing, expanding, and recording their stories in their home language. Children can also record stories in their home languages for later translation.

• Match text and spoken words with images to help children understand what they are listening to. Invite children to listen to favorite stories again and again to help build language and conceptual skills.

• Pronounce words slowly, clearly, and with expression when recording audio for digital versions of books.

• Make digital versions of children's stories and ideas available as slideshows or movie files for children to view.

How can computers support family involvement?

• Talk with families about appropriate use of computers with children. During a family night, introduce the programs you use and explain how they support learning.

• Inform families who do not have computers at home about local places to use them, such as the public library or a community center.

• Help children publish their stories/work and share classroom news and plans on a class website or blog. Family members near and far can review and find out

• Observe how children use the computer to know when to encourage them to move on to another activity and when to extend time for teachable moments.

• Plan times to share children's work. Read and discuss class books and stories created on the computer with the group.

How can I be sure all children are comfortable using the computer?

• Be sensitive to children who lack experience or are reluctant to use the computer. Provide plenty of support and time to practice, explore, and have fun using the computer. With focused assistance, children can become more comfortable.

• Assess a child's ability using a technology skills checklist, such as the one at http://umaine.edu/ccids/files/2010/07/TechSkillsChecklist.pdf.

• Adjust the computer volume, screen brightness, mouse sensitivity, and font size and type to suit the needs of individual children. Children can learn to make these adjustments.

• Offer headphones, touch screens, and other adaptive equipment to help all children access computer activities.

• Encourage tech-savvy children to become computer peer mentors. Model language and techniques so the mentors can build self-esteem and new relationships.

Resources for Learning More about Computer Use with Young Children

Clements, D., & S. Swaminathan. n.d. "Introducing Technology to Young Children." E-clips: Educational Video Clips for Early Childhood Professionals. Willimantic, CT: Eastern Connecticut State University. www.east ernct.edu/cece/e-clips_Technology.htm.

ISTE (International Society for Technology in Education). 2007. "NETS for Students: 2007 Profiles." www.iste. org/standards/nets-for-students/nets-for-students-2007-profiles.aspx.

NAEYC. 2012. Technology and Young Children Interest Forum website. www.techandyoungchildren.org.

NAEYC & Fred Rogers Center for Early Learning and Children's Media at Saint Vincent College. 2012. "Technology and Interactive Media as Tools in Early Childhood Programs Serving Children from Birth through Age 8." Joint position statement. Washington, DC: NAEYC. www.naeyc.org/files/naeyc/file/positions/PS_tech nology_WEB2.pdf.

NAEYC Technology and Young Children Interest Forum Members. "On Our Minds: Meaningful Technology Integration in Early Learning Environments." *Young Children* 63 (5): 48–50. www.naeyc.org/files/yc/ file/200809/OnOurMinds.pdf.

Thompson, S.K., & K. Williams. 2009. *Telling Stories with Photo Essays: A Guide for Pre-K–5 Teachers.* Thousand Oaks, CA: Corwin.

more about children's learning. Their comments or replies can also extend and enrich children's learning.

What can I do to increase my own knowledge and comfort with computers?

• Join online communities and explore free online resources, such as those offered by the NAEYC Technology and Young Children Interest Forum (www.techand youngchildren.org).

• Keep a printed copy of software program guides near the computer to use as a reference when questions arise. Also use the software programs' Help menus or video tutorials.

• Encourage children to show you when they discover something new about a software program or on a website.

• Learn more through technology workshops in your community (try the local library or adult education center), online tutorials, professional conferences, or a visit with a tech-savvy community member, such as a colleague or teenager.

Another motivational tool

Marco, who teaches dual language learners, notes, "Giving children an opportunity to draw pictures or use stamps and animations delights them and gives them the chance to express themselves when they can't yet express themselves in English. While working with Nadja on the computer, Abdi, whom I had never heard speak, came over and asked, 'It my turn?' When I told him that he could have another turn tomorrow, since it was almost time to go home and he already had a turn, he said, 'but not very long.' Wow, talk about being motivated to speak! The computer is a powerful motivator for this child!"

Preschool Children and Computers
Storytelling and Learning in a Digital Age

by Bonnie Blagojevic
and Suzanne Chevalier

This article describes how intentional planning of computer use in early childhood settings can provide young children with additional learning opportunities that can be beneficial and motivating. It provides classroom scenarios involving diverse learners, technology integration tips, suggestions for family involvement, and resources to extend learning about using computers with young children.

Key messages

1. Computers have unique characteristics that can offer young children additional ways to learn, tell and record stories, represent ideas, hear their stories read back to them, and share their work with others.
2. Early childhood educators need to consider children's interests, developmental stages, and abilities when planning computer-based activities to provide the appropriate level of challenge for every child. They should also provide supports so that diverse learners, including dual language learners and children with disabilities, can learn using the computer.
3. To use computers effectively with children, it is important for educators to learn about technology and carefully plan computer use. Educators need to consider where the computer is located, how it is introduced, and when and how to connect and integrate its use with other learning areas and priorities, such as increasing positive social interactions and play.

In your view

1. What are the three most important themes or key ideas in this article? If possible, compare your choices with those of others who have read the article.
2. How is the content of this article related to applicable early learning standards or other curriculum or program requirements?

Reflect and revisit your practice

1. What ideas in this article affirm your practice? What questions does this article raise about your teaching practices? What new approaches might you try?
2. What kind of supports do you and other teachers need to try out these new ideas?
3. What were your reactions to the photographs in this article? What do you think the children are learning? What could a teacher say to encourage the children's explorations?

Let's talk

1. How did you learn to use a computer? Was it formal instruction (in a classroom setting), informal (by friends or family members), or self-taught (hands-on exploration or tutorials)? How might your discoveries about your own learning preferences influence how you introduce computers to young children?
2. How does the joint position statement on technology and young children from NAEYC and the Fred Rogers Center align with your own beliefs about technology use with young children? How might your current use of technology change based on this position statement?
3. Do you currently plan how, when, and why you incorporate computers into your early childhood curriculum? How might this change after reading this article?
4. When you consider the children in your care, how might they enjoy and benefit from computer use as described in this article? How can computer use motivate and provide new access to learning for them, along with traditional options?

Steps you can take

1. After reviewing the article, particularly the bulleted lists and additional technology resources, develop a checklist to assess children's current computer use in your early childhood setting. From this checklist, select starting points for next steps and develop an action plan for incorporating computers into children's learning experiences.
2. Implement your action plan. Schedule times to review, revise, and update as needed.
3. Discuss what you have learned about young children's computer use with colleagues and families to support a coordinated approach for using technology with young children.

To increase your knowledge

ECETECH group—created by the NAEYC Technology & Young Children Interest Forum—on the social bookmarking site Diigo.com allows sharing and commenting on websites related to technology use with young children. http://groups.diigo.com/group/ecetech.

Freeman, N.K., & J. Somerindyke. 2001. "Social Play at the Computer: Preschoolers Scaffold and Support Peers' Computer Competence." *Information Technology in Childhood Education Annual, 2001*: 203–13.

Jackson, S. 2011. "Learning, Digital Media and Creative Play in Early Childhood." Spotlight. March 24. http://spotlight.macfound.org/featured-stories/entry/learning-digital-media-and-creative-play-in-early-childhood.

NAEYC and Fred Rogers Center. 2012. Support materials related to joint position statement on technology and young children: Examples of Effective Practice, Key Messages, Prerecorded Webcast, and Selected Resources. www.naeyc.org/content/technology-and-young-children.

The TEC (Technology in Early Childhood) Center at Erikson Institute. http://teccenter.erikson.edu.

Interactive Whiteboards in Early Childhood Mathematics

Strategies for Effective Implementation in Pre-K–Grade 3

Sandra M. Linder

© Gordon Studer

In a first grade classroom, children rotate through a variety of centers. A group of four children approaches the math center, which is stationed at the interactive whiteboard (IWB) this week. The children have been investigating money during the past few weeks, and this center provides an extension to these investigations. At the top of the IWB, there is a picture of a quarter labeled "25 Cents." Below it are pictures of pennies, nickels, and dimes that can be moved around the board and duplicated, depending on the activity. One child presses a picture of a horn, activating an audio file that asks the children to make 25 cents in a variety of ways using the coins on the IWB. The children work together to use the pennies, nickels, and dimes to create sets of 25.

Sandra M. Linder, PhD, is an assistant professor of early childhood mathematics education at Clemson University. Her research centers on improving preservice and in-service teacher quality and encouraging student success in early childhood mathematics.

Photos © Ellen B. Senisi.

naeyc® 2, 3

Teachers are using technological innovations—including interactive whiteboards—in pre-K–grade 3 classrooms across the country. An IWB is a wall-mounted, touch-sensitive flat screen. When connected to a computer (or another electronic device) and a projector, it displays enlarged instructional content (such as a math word problem, pictures or graphics, or an excerpt from a story). Teachers and children can manipulate this content. Many early childhood teachers are incorporating this technology in their mathematics instruction. This article will help educators use IWBs and other technologies in ways that coincide with best practices in early childhood math instruction. It also shares examples of how to integrate other digital tools into mathematics instruction.

Math lessons in early childhood should use child-centered practices to develop children's conceptual understanding of a variety of topics. However, teachers sometimes use IWBs merely to complete electronic worksheets or to show examples of problems to be solved during the lesson. By making small tweaks to their approach, teachers can alter the focus of a task to promote children's active learning. For example, a second grade teacher might bring up place value in the number representing the day on the calendar ("Today is January 31. How many ones are in 31? How many tens are in 31?"). Instead of ending the discussion here and showing a representation of the tens and ones on the IWB, have the children form small groups and draw a representation of the place values for the 3 and the 1. Ask the groups to share their representations by redrawing them on the IWB.

The current literature on interactive white boards is limited; however, there are examples of early childhood teachers incorporating IWBs effectively. Murcia (2010) relates a case study describing how elementary school teachers integrate IWBs into their science curriculum. Murcia's findings show that the use of multimodal representations—such as tables and graphics children can manipulate on the IWB—increase the richness of lesson plans and the collaboration and communication among students. In a study of kindergartners working with an IWB and other forms of technology during math lessons on fractions, Goodwin (2008) finds that children who use these forms of interactive technology have more complex understandings of fractions than children in settings where the technology is not incorporated into lessons.

Essential characteristics of early childhood mathematics lessons

The table below describes characteristics that should be present in every early childhood math lesson. These characteristics reflect the process standards of the National Council of Teachers of Mathematics (2006). Although the list does not include all effective practices, it can be helpful when designing mathematics instruction. By including these practices in every lesson, you can help children be active, rather than passive, learners of math concepts.

Essential Characteristics of Early Childhood Mathematics Lessons

Building communities and communication	Create activities that build a **community of learners** in your classroom. Have children work collaboratively. Structure discussions so that interactions occur between children, between you and the children, and between the children and you (meaning that they ask you questions or pose thoughts rather than you eliciting information from them). For example, ask children multiple open-ended questions as they work together on a math task, and incorporate time in each lesson for whole-group discussions so that children can reflect on their task and describe their strategies for solving it. Structure your lessons so that all children feel ownership of a task and so they can all engage in the discussion.
Making connections	Make **connections** between mathematics and other content areas, and between mathematics and real-world situations. Children need to understand why they are engaging in tasks. Insert discussions about math concepts into informal situations, such as during free play or while setting the table for snack or lunch. When math concepts are meaningful for children, they can see the value of mathematics and relate the information to what they already understand.
Representing understanding	Provide opportunities for children to **represent their thinking** in a variety of ways. For example, ask kindergartners to show their strategies for breaking up (decomposing) the number 5 into groups, using both pictures and numbers, as well as discussion. Ask second-graders to show their strategies for solving a two-digit addition problem in pictures, numbers, and written sentences. These different representations help children move from concrete to abstract understandings.
Exploring with materials	Provide opportunities for children to use different **materials** or **manipulatives** to help solve math tasks. Remember, mathematics instruction should not be just hands-on; it should be *minds-on*—meaning that children should use the manipulatives as a tool to help represent their understanding. Instead of asking them to use materials in prescribed ways, allow for flexibility in how children decide to use the materials.
Child-centered tasks	Design math **tasks** in which children can approach a challenge in a variety of ways. There should be no one way to solve a problem. Avoid telling children how you would solve the problem. Allow them time to explore the task, which will give you an opportunity to ask questions and understand and build on their thinking.

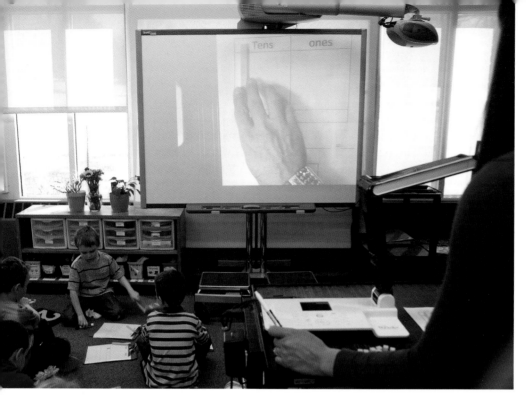

Following this discussion, Ms. Carlin gives each child an opportunity to count a set of elephants and tell how many there are in all. The children go to the IWB and use their fingers to drag the elephants from one side of the board to the other to represent the action of counting, and to demonstrate their understanding of one-to-one correspondence. Once they have all taken a turn with the IWB, they work with a partner to group and count sets of plastic animals in different ways.

Integrating technology and mathematics using an IWB

When building math lessons around the essential characteristics in the table, it is important that the IWB not be the only tool children interact with during lessons. The best way to use an IWB is either before or after a small-group task in which children use concrete materials, such as plastic cubes that children can link together and pull apart. Use the IWB to introduce a topic, to stimulate discussion, or to connect math concepts to real-world situations. Avoid using the IWB to show children how to complete the task.

The following are examples from practicing teachers showing how to incorporate an IWB in each early childhood mathematics content area (number and operations, data analysis, measurement, algebra, and geometry).

Number and operations

In a pre-K classroom (with 4-year-olds), Ms. Carlin is teaching counting skills and the concept of cardinality (understanding a set of objects as a total quantity or sum rather than as individual parts). Children gather on the rug in front of an IWB where Ms. Carlin displays pictures of 10 elephants, all slightly different (in terms of height, color, trunk length). She asks the children to talk about the different ways to count the elephants (count them all, count just the gray ones, count just the tall ones). They then discuss how to tell if an elephant meets the criterion set by the group.

Ms. Carlin: How can you tell if this elephant is tall or short?

Quoila: We counted them by color.
Phin: We counted them by number of legs.
LaMont: We put them in groups of two and then counted by twos.

Following every turn of counting, the pairs draw each set on a piece of paper and label it with a number.

Data analysis in kindergarten

When introducing the parts of a pictograph in a kindergarten class, Ms. Nocenti uses the interactive whiteboard to do a class survey of favorite types of apples (red, green, or other). Children begin the lesson on the carpet in front of the IWB, where the teacher holds up a bundle of apples and asks the children to come up with questions to ask about them.

Ms. Nocenti: What are some questions we can ask about these apples?
Malik: How big are they?
Sera: How many apples are there in the bundle?
Marzuk: Which one do you like best?
Matt: What is your favorite one?

From the list of questions generated by the children, they choose "What is your favorite type of apple?" to explore. Ms. Nocenti uses this question to guide the creation of, and conversation about, a pictograph on the IWB.

The best way to use an IWB is either before or after a small-group task in which children use concrete materials.

Ms. Nocenti: How can we find out what everyone's favorite type of apple is?

Matt: We can each take a bite of apple and then choose.

Malik: We can raise our hand when you say the type we like best.

Sera: We can draw a picture of the apple we like best.

Throughout this discussion, Ms. Nocenti records on the IWB children's responses about ways to learn which type of apple they like best. After recording everyone's responses, she asks children to draw a picture of their favorite apple. Ms. Nocenti then calls each child up to the board to draw a circle (in the appropriate color), representing his or her choice. The drawings are scattered on the IWB, with no apparent method of organizing the data.

Ms. Nocenti: Now that you have each decided which type of apple you like best, how can we organize this information so it is easy to see?

Matt: We can put all of our apple drawings together and then put [same-color apples] next to each other.

Following this conversation, each group receives a bundle of apples and comes up with a different question to ask about them, creates a pictograph on paper to represent their findings, and shares their graph with the class. As the groups share their graphs, Ms. Nocenti re-creates them on the IWB. As she records them on the IWB, the whole class gains an understanding of how each group created its pictograph. In addition, she saves each re-created pictograph from the IWB so that she has documentation of the children's thinking.

Measurement in first grade

Money is often a difficult concept for young children to grasp. In his first grade class, Mr. Jimenez introduces a lesson on pennies, nickels, and dimes by having a picture of each coin on the IWB. The children compare and contrast the characteristics of the coins and create a class list on the IWB of each coin's attributes.

Mr. Jimenez: How are each of these coins similar?

Annie: They all can be used to buy things.

Niranjan: They are all round.

Tasunke: They all have faces on them.

Mr. Jimenez: How are each of these coins different?

Niranjan: They are different sizes. This one is bigger than that one.

Akiko: The dime is ten cents, the nickel is five cents, the penny is only one.

Annie: The penny is a different color.

Niranjan: You can get more with the dime.

After the class creates its list, the children break up into small groups and create money amounts using as many coin combinations as possible. Following this task, the children gather back at the IWB and each group dem-

> **As the groups share their graphs, Ms. Nocenti re-creates them on the IWB. As she records them on the IWB, the whole class gains an understanding of how each group created its pictograph.**

onstrates how they used a combination of coins to make a certain money amount, using their fingers to drag each coin into a set that represents the amount.

Akiko: We used two dimes and two nickels to make 30 cents. Then we used 10 pennies and two dimes to make 30 cents. Then we used 15 pennies and three nickels to make 30 cents.

Mr. Jimenez facilitates a whole-group discussion by asking questions about the children's decision making when choosing certain coin combinations, and by having children compare these decisions to their own thinking. For example, when Akiko describes the three ways that her group made 30 cents, Mr. Jimenez asks the rest of the groups to share other ways to make 30 cents. Mr. Jimenez develops the center activity described at the beginning of this article as an extension to this lesson.

Algebra in second grade

In a lesson on generalizing patterns, second grade teacher Ms. Romita uses the IWB during the reflection period following a math task. Children begin the lesson by discussing the different repeating patterns they see in their classroom and whether they had seen any of those repeating patterns outside of school. For example, one child sees a color pattern of stripes on a classmate's T-shirt and then recognizes that the same pattern is present in a bed of flowers in the yard.

The children then work in pairs to create the same repeating pattern in three different ways (with a picture, with pattern blocks, and with movement). For example, one pair creates a pattern of red square, yellow hexagon, green triangle with pattern blocks, and then represents this pattern with a star, a cat, and a heart. Once they create these representations, they use movement to create a third representation of the same pattern with hop on two feet, clap, and raising both hands above their heads. Next, they write a general statement about each of the three representations.

Following this task, the children gather at the interactive whiteboard, where Ms. Romita has each pair share one of their representations. The pairs come up to the

The children gather back at the IWB and each group demonstrates how they used a combination of coins to make a certain money amount, using their fingers to drag each coin into a set that represents the amount.

IWB and show the movement representation of their pattern and then draw the picture version of the pattern on the IWB. The teacher then asks a child from outside the pair to make another representation of the pattern using color tiles on the IWB.

Ms. Romita: How did you represent your pattern?

Gwen: We used sounds. We did clap, stomp, stomp, clap; clap, stomp, stomp, clap.

Ms. Romita: Then what did you do?

Jorge: We made the same pattern with triangle, square, square, triangle.

Ms. Romita: Boys and girls, how can you use the color tiles to show this pattern?

Ciria: Well, you could put the yellow tile first, then put the red tile, and then another red tile, and then a yellow tile, and then keep going.

Geometry in third grade

In a third grade lesson on intersecting and parallel lines, Ms. Talamantes uses the IWB during the first part of the lesson to show pictures of intersecting and parallel lines in the real world, including photos of roads and buildings in their community. Children draw over the pictures—using the interactive pen that comes with the IWB—to show where the parallel or intersecting lines occur. She asks children to explain the differences between the examples, which eventually leads the children to come up with their own definitions for intersecting lines and parallel lines.

Ms. Talamantes: How are these two lines here and these two lines here similar?

Malik: They are all straight.

Soo Jin: They are on the edges of the buildings.

Ms. Talamantes: How are they different?

Yasmine: These cross and these don't.

Soo Jin: The ones that cross make a corner on the building.

Malik: The ones that don't cross on either side of the building are connected by another line that crosses over both of them.

Following this whole-group discussion, children work in pairs to draw a picture of a space in their school (for example, the lunchroom, playground, gym, classroom). After they draw their picture, each pair writes a description of their space on paper, giving attention specifically to where they found parallel or intersecting lines. During the week, the children take turns visiting the spaces to determine if there are any examples they had missed.

Other technologies for teaching math

The following are examples of other forms of technology that teachers can use to enhance mathematics lessons—with or without an IWB. Remember to include the essential characteristics (see p. 23) in your math lessons when implementing these examples.

Virtual manipulatives

Rosen and Hoffman (2009) define virtual manipulatives as "interactive, web-based, computer-generated images of objects that children can manipulate on the computer screen" (26). They are available to teachers for free through a variety of websites (see "Resources," p. 28). These manipulatives often look similar to the concrete forms you may already use in your classroom (for example, place-value blocks, pattern blocks, color tiles). However, if you don't have access to such materials, virtual manipulatives are an option.

Websites with virtual manipulatives often offer specific tasks for children to complete. Teachers can easily incorporate these tasks into a math center when an IWB is not available. Invite children to work in pairs at a computer to complete a math task using virtual manipulatives. For example, on the National Library of Virtual Manipulatives website (http://nlvm.usu.edu), pairs can access an *attribute train,* enabling them to identify and complete patterns by analyzing attributes of shapes. Often, these tasks require children to simply answer the questions. (For example, if a task involves using place-value blocks to solve an addition problem, the website might not require the children to describe their strategy for using the blocks.) Enhance these tasks by asking the pairs of children to create another example or to represent their strategies for solving the original problem on a separate piece of paper. For example, after pairs interact with the attribute train, have one child in the pair create her own example of an attribute train on paper and then ask the other child to complete the pattern. Once the pattern is complete, have the pair switch roles. After all of the children have interacted with the virtual manipulatives at the mathematics center, gather the class as a whole group to discuss their strategies.

With an IWB, you can optimize the use of virtual manipulatives by combining them with concrete manipulatives. For example, during a lesson on attributes of shapes, ask children to form small groups and use concrete manipulatives, such as pattern blocks or tangrams (seven individual shapes that, when combined without overlapping, can form a variety of larger shapes), to make a representation of an animal or a monster. Allow the children to design their own representations rather than telling them what to make. Following this exploration, gather the children together and have them share their representations using the virtual manipulatives on the IWB. Display the virtual manipulatives and ask children to click and drag the shapes to re-create their representation. During discussion, children can explore how to use more shapes to create the same animal. Teachers can also use other computer programs, such as Kidspiration (a free trial is available to download, but the program must be purchased) or Microsoft Word (by inserting shapes into a document), to create their own virtual manipulatives.

Webquests

Webquests—Internet-based explorations in which children visit teacher-selected websites to solve a problem or complete a task—are a great way to make connections in mathematics lessons. A variety of websites enable teachers to easily create webquests for any content area for free (see "Resources," p. 28) For classrooms without IWBs, children can pursue webquests on computers in math centers as long as they can easily navigate the sites. Instructions should be succinct, and links should be easy to find so children do not spend more time figuring out the technology than they do working on the math task. Ideally, children work in pairs or small groups to complete the webquest, and they have opportunities to make connections between the webquest and the classroom. For example, if children are completing a webquest on identifying three-dimensional shapes on various websites, ask them to identify the same shapes in their classroom and to represent them in drawings.

Incorporate webquests into whole-group lessons in classrooms with IWBs by developing a math task that can be solved only by exploring a variety of websites as a group. Ms. Romita developed a webquest for her second grade class that connected mathematics and social studies by following an explorer's travels as he visited different communities around the world. Children explore the sites he visited and, as a group, figure out how far he traveled. To encourage more child-to-child interaction, have children work together in smaller groups during the lesson to complete the tasks included in the webquest (such as adding together the miles from one location to another) and then meet back as a whole group to discuss and compare findings.

Recordings and photographs

It can be difficult to formatively assess all children as they work together during a math lesson. Use a video or voice recorder to capture discussions and interactions while children engage in math tasks. The information gathered from these tools will help inform your assessment and planning for the subsequent lesson. A video or voice recorder can also enhance a lesson by providing a way for children to record their thoughts so they can think about them later. For example, in a second grade lesson on addition with regrouping, children work in groups to solve a word problem, showing three solving strategies (pictures, words, and numbers). Following this task, the teacher gathers children for a whole-group discussion of the different strategies. The teacher records the discussion, but there is time for only half the class to share their strategies. The next day, the teacher plays back the recording so the children can remember the discussion. Often, due to time restrictions, the reflection component—which is critical to mathematics lessons—is shortened. By recording their thinking, children can return to this information later to help refocus them on the task.

In classrooms with an IWB, use a video or voice recorder to document assessment data from children in small groups, and then play the recording during whole-group discussions at the IWB. Allow children to watch another small group working, for example, to build a structure with three-dimensional shapes. After watching the small group work, the teacher can ask all the children specific questions about how the small group completed the task, helping children think about mathematical processes. For example, kindergartners building structures with three-dimensional shapes watch a video of another group building a castle and begin to identify castles they had seen in the real world or on television. One of the children in the video struggles to find a place for a sphere, and as the children watch him try out various spots, they predict whether the

sphere will fall and volunteer alternative suggestions for where to place it.

Digital photography can also enhance instruction in mathematics. Using a digital camera, children in pairs can collect data during mathematical tasks. For example, if children take a pattern walk (identifying examples of repeating or growing patterns as they walk around the school), have them use a digital camera with their partner to capture examples of these patterns along the way. Digital photographs can easily be shown on an IWB or a computer, or printed and displayed on a board as a means to encourage whole-group discussion and make math connections to the real world. For example, displaying pictures of flowers that children grew in a community garden can encourage a discussion on symmetry.

Conclusion

Technology can be a vital tool in enhancing mathematics instruction for young children. However, if a teacher is standing next to the interactive whiteboard throughout an entire mathematics lesson, or if children's only interaction with an IWB is to come up one at a time to answer a question, then it is not being used in the most effective manner. When early childhood teachers design lessons by integrating the forms of technology discussed here with the essential characteristics for teaching early childhood mathematics, children are more likely to develop conceptual understandings and positive dispositions toward mathematics at a young age.

References

Goodwin, K. 2008. "The Impact of Interactive Multimedia on Kindergarten Students' Representations of Fractions." *Issues in Educational Research* 18 (2): 103–117.

Murcia, K. 2010. "Multi-Modal Representations in Primary Science: What's Offered by Interactive Whiteboard Technology." *Teaching Science* 56 (1): 23–29.

National Council of Teachers of Mathematics (NCTM). 2006. *Curriculum Focal Points for Prekindergarten through Grade 8 Mathematics.* Reston, VA: Author. www.nctm.org/standards/content.aspx?id=16909.

After watching the small group work, the teacher can ask all the children specific questions about how the small group completed the task, helping children think about mathematical processes.

Rosen, D., & J. Hoffman. 2009. "Integrating Concrete and Virtual Manipulatives in Early Childhood Mathematics." *Young Children* 64 (3): 26–33.

Resources

Websites offering virtual manipulatives

Illuminations. National Council of Teachers of Mathematics site featuring pre-K–12 lesson plans and activities related to all content areas. The activities link provides free access to early childhood virtual manipulatives. **http://illuminations.nctm.org**

Kidspiration. Software designed for grades K–5. Originally a language arts program, it now includes a mathematics component, allowing teachers to use pictures, text, and numbers to create math problems and tasks. A free trial version is available, but eventually the program must be purchased. **www.inspiration.com/Kidspiration**

Math Forum. Reviews and links to websites that provide virtual manipulatives or sample lessons using virtual manipulatives. **http://mathforum.org**

National Library of Virtual Manipulatives. Virtual manipulatives for all pre-K–12 math content areas (number and operations, algebra, geometry, measurement, data analysis, and probability). A free trial version is available. **http://nlvm.usu.edu**

Websites for webquests

Discovery Education. Provides Mac and PC templates for creating webquests, plus information on creating and implementing webquests. Sample webquests from practicing teachers are included. **http://school.discovery education.com/schrockguide/webquest/webquest.html**

Education World. Features a detailed description of qualities and components to include in a webquest, plus downloadable webquest templates and links to other webquest resources. **www.educationworld.com/a_tech/tech/tech011.shtml**

TeacherWeb. Information on using webquests across all content areas, and a template for creating webquests. Sample webquests are also provided. **www.teacherweb.com**

Interactive Whiteboards in Early Childhood Mathematics

Strategies for Effective Implementation in Pre-K–Grade 3

by Sandra M. Linder

This article describes the ways in which early childhood teachers can effectively integrate technology into mathematics learning experiences, particularly through the use of interactive whiteboards (IWBs). Classroom vignettes featuring the effective use of interactive whiteboards and examples of other forms of technology to enhance mathematics lessons are provided.

Key messages

1. Using interactive whiteboards as part of child-centered mathematics instruction can help pre-K through third grade children develop a conceptual understanding of a variety of key mathematical concepts.
2. The essential characteristics of early childhood mathematics teaching and learning include opportunities to build learning communities; make connections between mathematics and other content areas, and between mathematics and real-world situations; represent understanding in a variety of ways; explore materials; and solve problems using a variety of approaches.
3. Mathematics instruction with technology is most effective when children participate as active learners and when used before or after small group work in which children use concrete materials.

In your view

1. What are the three most important themes or key ideas in this article? If possible, compare your choices with those of others who have read the article.
2. How is the content of this article related to applicable early learning standards or other curriculum or program requirements?

Reflect and revisit your practice

1. What ideas in this article affirm your practice? What questions does the article raise about your teaching practices? What new approaches might you try?
2. What kinds of supports do you and other teachers need to try out these new ideas?

Let's talk

1. What are your childhood memories of mathematics learning? Did your teachers integrate technology into their instruction, and how do you think this influenced your learning?
2. How do you currently use technology in your mathematics experiences? Do the activities you provide with technology reflect the essential characteristics of early childhood mathematics instruction? How?
3. How do you think the children you teach will respond to the activities shared in this article?
4. How has the information in this article changed the way you think about incorporating technology into mathematics teaching and learning? Which strategies do you plan to use in the classroom?

Steps you can take

1. Develop a mathematics lesson that integrates the use of interactive whiteboards or the other technologies featured in the article—for example using an interactive whiteboard during a lesson on counting or using virtual manipulatives in a mathematics center.
2. Implement and document children's reactions to the learning experience. How did the use of technology influence the children's learning?
3. Reflect and share on the teaching and learning. What changes would you make for the next lesson? What did you learn about using technology to promote mathematical learning?

Glossary

Interactive whiteboard (IWB)—a wall-mounted, touch-sensitive flat screen that displays enlarged instructional content when connected to a computer or other electronic device and a projector.

Virtual manipulatives—"interactive, web-based computer-generated images of objects that children can manipulate on the computer screen" (Rosen & Hoffman 2009, 26).

Webquests—Internet-based explorations in which children visit teacher-selected websites to solve a problem or complete a task.

To increase your knowledge

Copley, J.V. 2010. *The Young Child and Mathematics.* 2nd ed. Washington, DC: NAEYC.

Craig, D.V. 2000. "Technology, Math, and the Early Learner: Models for Learning." *Early Childhood Education Journal* 27 (3): 179–84.

Early Childhood Technology blog. http://earlychildhoodtech.edublogs.org.

Suh, J., C. Johnston, & J. Douds. 2008. "Enhancing Mathematical Learning in a Technology-Rich Environment." *Teaching Children Mathematics* 15 (3): 235–41.

Reference

Rosen, D., & J. Hoffman. 2009. "Integrating Concrete and Virtual Manipulatives in Early Childhood Mathematics." *Young Children* 64 (3): 26–33.

Touch Tablet Surprises

A Preschool Teacher's Story

© Gordon Studer

Rena Shifflet, Cheri Toledo, and Cassandra Mattoon

A year and a half ago, Rena, Cheri, and Cassandra were introduced to each other by a colleague because they shared an interest in exploring the impact newer technologies have on learning in early childhood classrooms. They meet regularly to share ideas and information on how to incorporate tablets using best practices. Cassandra's preschool classroom serves as a natural environment for them to test their ideas. This article describes a collaborative effort. The authors are conducting additional research on the use of technology with preschool children.

Cassandra never thought about having the children in her preschool classroom use touch tablets until she was approached by the technology coordinator for her school. She is guided by her belief that hands-on learning experiences are essential and any technology must correspond with developmentally appropriate practice so children can explore and learn about their world. When she found herself with four touch tablets, she wondered what kind of learning experiences these tools could give the young learners.

Cassandra experimented with a touch tablet and several free applications (apps) before realizing she needed to see a young child interacting with one. She enlisted her 4-year-old nephew and watched as he easily maneuvered his way around the touch tablet interface and its apps. He seemed to know instinctively about moving his finger on the screen to manipulate the apps. Without any instruction from Cassandra, he even discovered activities on the apps that she had not found. His reaction to the touch tablet fueled her curiosity about using it as a learning tool in her early childhood classroom.

Rena Shifflet, EdD, is an assistant professor at Illinois State University in Normal, Illinois. Prior to taking a position in higher education, Rena worked as an elementary classroom teacher and district technology coordinator for over 30 years. Her research work includes the study of preservice and in-service teacher technology use for pre-K–8.

Cheri Toledo, EdD, is an associate professor of educational technology in the curriculum and instruction department at Illinois State University. Her research interests are strategic uses of current and emerging technologies to increase effective teaching and learning.

Cassandra Mattoon, BS in early childhood education, is the preschool teacher at Thomas Metcalf Lab School at Illinois State University. Cassandra is conducting research on the use of tablets in early childhood education settings.

Photos courtesy of Cassandra Mattoon.

naeyc ® 2, 3

Cassandra, an early childhood teaching veteran, describes herself as a neophyte technology user. So, adding a cutting-edge technology like touch tablets caused her some concern. For Cassandra, and many early childhood educators, preschool is a time for children to experience real life in play, use their imaginations, and engage in multiple hands-on experiences as they construct their own understandings of the world. Teachers take great care in designing stimulating learning environments while considering individual needs and differences. It is this intentionality that sets the foundation for developmentally appropriate practice (NAEYC & Fred Rogers Center 2012). When educators add technology as an instructional tool, the interface may be different, but the principles remain the same.

The touch tablet is just one of many tools used to expand children's learning experiences (Guernsey 2010). It is important for teachers to evaluate every instructional tool for its effectiveness in context. There are benefits and challenges to each (Cooper 2005), and it is the educator's responsibility to determine when each is advantageous to children's learning and development (NAEYC & Fred Rogers Center 2012).

When educators add technology as an instructional tool, the interface may be different, but the principles remain the same.

Some educators, researchers, and parents stress that children already spend too much time in front of television and computer screens (Plowman, McPake, & Stephen 2010), so why add more technology during the school day? This line of thinking led Cassandra to ask herself what role technology should play in a quality preschool program. She also understood that NAEYC and the Fred Rogers Center (2012) recommend that teachers be willing to learn about new technologies, evaluate their purpose, and observe children's use of the tools to make informed decisions about how technology is used in the classroom.

Introducing the new technology

Concern about the negative impact that computer use has on children's social interactions in the classroom is a long-standing issue in education circles (Barnes & Hill 1983; Finegan & Austin 2002). With this in mind, Cassandra slowly integrated the touch tablets by first introducing a single device for a group of children. She began by showing the tablet to the entire group during circle time and discussing how children could use it. The children then dispersed to play in a variety of centers. Cassandra

remained on the rug and worked with a small group of children who were interested in exploring the tablet. Four children then moved to the library center to work together on the tablet. As the week progressed, all of the children had used the tablet. Once she was satisfied with their interactions, Cassandra gave the children two tablets, eventually making all four touch tablets available in the library center. She hoped that without enough tablets for individual play, the children would learn to use them cooperatively.

As Cassandra introduced the touch tablets into her classroom activities, she encountered four surprises. The first came as she sought the answer to the question, "Would using these devices encourage isolated play?"

Surprise 1: Cooperation!

From the first time she introduced the touch tablets, Cassandra found the children interacting cooperatively. Her observations supported Kumtepe (2006), who notes that rather than fostering social isolation, children's computer use increases social skills. Children who use computers more frequently and at a more proficient level demonstrated more social skill gains and fewer problem behaviors in kindergarten.

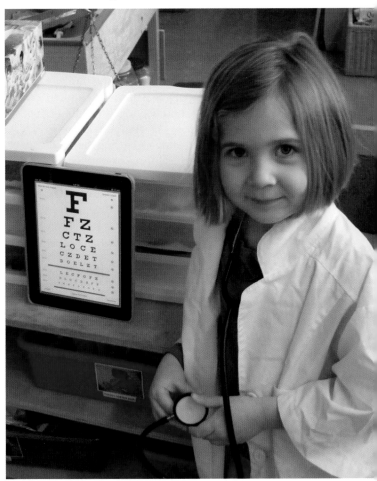

One day, Cassandra observed four children sitting around one touch tablet, playing a memory match app. She thought to herself, "Maybe this technology is OK and can encourage cooperative play." Contrary to her initial concern, she discovered that the children rarely used the touch tablets in isolation. Even when four children were each using a tablet, they huddled together, interacting, teaching, and learning from one another. On one occasion, when four children were each using their own tablet, she purposefully had them sit three to four feet apart. Within moments they had worked their way back into their huddle and resumed their collaborative interactions. The impact on their language skills as they exchanged comments and suggestions was apparent. Children were sharing ideas, helping each other find apps, and asking each other questions.

The tablets also allowed for more collaboration than traditional art tools. Many apps encourage creativity, such as some of the drawing apps that were popular with the children. They created pictures related to a unit of study, putting much thought and time into the design of their pictures. While the children used the drawing apps, Cassandra discovered the second surprise.

Children were sharing ideas, helping each other find apps, and asking each other questions.

Surprise 2: Collaboration!

Cassandra found the children working collaboratively to design and create their pictures. In traditional art centers, children rarely work on one piece of art together—each child walks away with his or her own piece of art. With the touch tablet, the children fed off of one another's suggestions and created art together. Three children began to make a picture about fall. One child drew a fall tree. A second child said, "I will add the squirrel." They then suggested that the third child add a bird in the tree. Cassandra heard them say, "Look what we did; we did this together; we were a team." Not only were they proud of their work of art, but they also took great pride in their collaborative effort—quite a contrast from the more common single-ownership attitudes seen with traditional, nontechnology-based artwork.

As she continued to think through the use of technology with preschoolers, Cassandra asked more questions: How much time should she allocate to the devices? Will the children be so enamored with the technology that they won't want to engage in other activities?

Surprise 3: Digital citizenship!

At first, the children's natural curiosity promoted their desire to use and play with a new toy. As Vygotsky (1978) states, "A child's greatest achievements are possible in play" (100). Play is part of the natural learning process and one way young children construct meaning. As the children used the tablets and explored the possibilities, some children seemed more fixated on using the technology than others—they just couldn't get enough time with the tablets. However, some of the initial newness wore off as the tablets became a natural part of the classroom environment. Cassandra found that the children still wanted to engage in other hands-on activities in the classroom, and they willingly and naturally moved on to other activities. Her observations support the idea that technology should not replace other forms of active exploration, and when used appropriately and responsibly, technology is another tool for teaching and learning (Fisch et al. 2002; Yelland 2005; NAEYC & Fred Rogers Center 2012). An important goal is a healthy balance between activities with and without technology.

Initial experience and reactions

As the children continuously used the touch tablets, Cassandra remained wary that they might prefer the tablet and their apps to parallel real-life experiences. She asked herself, "Would a child understand that what he was seeing and doing on the tablet is only a representation of the actual real-world event?" She decided to create an opportunity for them to experience both real and virtual cookie making. They read stories about cookies, watched a short video about a bakery, and then set up a bakery in the dramatic play area of the classroom. They were excited when the day to bake real cookies finally arrived!

Cassandra used a document camera (digital overhead projector) to demonstrate how to use the cookie app to virtually mix dough and decorate cookies. The children then went to centers. In the library center, children continued to read books about cookies. In the writing area, children created signs to promote and sell the cookies. In dramatic play, they assumed the roles of bakery employees and customers. Jill took a "customer's order" with the tablet and shared it with the bakers. Another group mixed the "dough" in the sand/water table, while the cookie decorators added the final touches.

In the cooking area, each child added an ingredient and mixed the batter, first using the application and then with the actual ingredients. Using his finger, Marcus touched the egg to make it crack, and the egg fell neatly into the virtual bowl without any pieces of shell. Then Marcus cracked a real egg and dumped it into the actual bowl. Cassandra asked him how it felt when he cracked the egg on the touch tablet and when he cracked a real egg. "It's hard. It's sticky. It's not easy to crack an egg!" Marcus quickly learned that cracking a real egg was nothing like a gentle finger tap on the tablet. As each ingredient was measured and added—into both the virtual and the real bowl—the children said, "You can't smell it on the computer." "It's hard to stir the dough." "The butter really is sticky." Cassandra asked, "Is making cookies on the tablet anything like making real cookies?" A unanimous "No!" was followed by "And you don't really get to eat the cookies you make on there!"

Surprise 4: Connection to the real world!

The children could tell real from virtual, and they still wanted to engage in the real-life experiences. This activity reinforced what Cassandra already knew about developmentally appropriate practice—children still need and desire real-life experiences. The touch tablet technology helped reinforce cookie-making steps and the children's vocabulary—a perfect example of using a technology tool to support and enhance a traditional learning experience, one that connects real-world experiences with the digital world (Yelland 2005).

As the preschoolers continued their work with the tablets in various center activities, they seemed quite at ease with this technology. This was illustrated when Rena observed a child using the cookie app. Billy selected the dough and rolled it out. He chose a cookie cutter, pressed it into the virtual dough, and instantly saw that the dough was not large enough for the cutter. Without any hesitation, he tapped the back button to get to the previous screen and rerolled the dough. When he was satisfied with the size of the dough, he went to the next screen and instead of selecting the same large cookie cutter, he chose a smaller cutter that easily fit his dough. Amazed by Billy's ability to quickly and efficiently solve his problem, Rena asked if he had ever used this particular app before. Without stopping his cookie decorating, Billy said he did

Questions to Consider when Deciding to Use a Technology Tool or Application

- How can I incorporate technology into my current curriculum in developmentally appropriate ways?
- How am I enhancing the learning experience with the use of technology?
- What am I giving up to make time for the use of technology?
- How can children learn from the technology used for this activity?
- Am I helping to close the learning gap in experiences between the children in my classroom who have and have not previously used technology?
- Is the objective to reinforce or teach a skill? Does the technology activity effectively help me reach this objective, or is there a more appropriate way to reinforce or teach this skill?
- Have I properly evaluated the app for its appropriateness in an educational setting, using the criteria I would use for other games, books, and toys?

When educators are intentional and selective in its use, technology can enhance early childhood education.

not have a touch tablet at home, and this was the first time he had used the cookie app. Rena's observation supports the position of NAEYC and the Fred Rogers Center (2012) that technology can and should provide opportunities for children to be creative, solve problems, think, and make decisions.

Observations

Cassandra has come a long way in the short time she has been using touch tablets in her classroom—from helping the children hold the device for fear it might drop and break, to letting them touch the screen while making cookie dough. Many educators resist using technology out of concern that it is not developmentally appropriate for young children. However, when educators are intentional and selective in its use, technology can enhance early childhood education (Yelland 2005; NAEYC & Fred Rogers Center 2012). According to Yelland (2005), when such technologies are embedded in the curriculum, "young children can not only experience concepts that were previously well beyond that expected of them, but that they could deploy sophisticated strategies and work collaboratively with others in new and dynamic ways" (224).

As early childhood educators, we understand that most preschoolers are at ease with technology: it has been continually present in their lives, and they are growing up with it. It is not possible to deny who they are and how they fit into the digital world in which they live (Zevenbergen 2007). Cassandra stated at the end of the year, "After experimenting with technology in my own classroom, my question is not should I be using it, but how, in what capacity, and how often. I've moved past the question of *if*."

Applications For Both Android™ and Apple iPod® Touch Tablets

Dr. Seuss Books—Classic interactive stories by Dr. Seuss.

Monkey Preschool Lunchbox—Activities related to colors, letters, counting, shapes, differences, and matching.

Shape Builder Preschool Puzzle—Variety of puzzles, including letters, animals, vehicles, instruments, and food. When a puzzle is complete, it shows a photo of the item and the sound it makes, if applicable.

Super Why—Activities based on characters from the PBS Kids series, SUPER WHY. Children practice alphabet, rhyming, spelling, writing, and reading skills.

References

Barnes, B.J. & S. Hill. 1983. "Should Young Children Work with Microcomputers: Logo before Lego?" *The Computing Teacher* 10 (9): 11–14.

Cooper, L.Z. 2005. "Developmentally Appropriate Digital Environments for Young Children." *Library Trends* 54 (2): 286–302. www.ideals.illinois.edu/bitstream/handle/2142/3477/Cooper_Developmentally.pdf?sequence=2.

Finegan, C., & N.J. Austin. 2002. "Developmentally Appropriate Technology for Young Children." *Information Technology in Childhood Education Annual* 2002 (1): 87–102. Association for the Advancement of Computing in Education (AACE).

Fisch, S.M., J.S. Shulman, A. Akerman, & G.A. Levin. 2002. "Reading between the Pixels: Parent-Child Interaction While Reading Online Storybooks." *Early Education and Development* 13 (4): 435–51.

Guernsey, L. 2010. "Screens, Kids and the NAEYC Position Statement." *Early Ed Watch blog* (New America Foundation). http://earlyed.newamerica.net/blogposts/2010/screens_kids_and_the_naeyc_ position_statement-35103.

Kumtepe, A.T. 2006. "The Effects of Computers on Kindergarten Children's Social Skills." *The Turkish Online Journal of Educational Technology* 5 (4): 52–57.

NAEYC & Fred Rogers Center for Early Learning and Children's Media at Saint Vincent College. 2012. "Technology and Interactive Media as Tools in Early Childhood Programs Serving Children from Birth through Age 8." Joint position statement. Washington, DC: NAEYC. www.naeyc.org/files/naeyc/file/positions/PS_technology_WEB2.pdf.

Plowman, L., J. McPake, & C. Stephen. 2010. "The Technologisation of Childhood? Young Children and Technology in the Home." *Children & Society* 24 (1): 63–74.

Vygotsky, L.S. 1978. *Mind in Society: The Development of Higher Psychological Processes.* Cambridge, MA: Harvard University Press.

Yelland, N. 2005. "The Future Is Now: A Review of the Literature on the Use of Computers in Early Childhood Education (1994–2004)." *AACE Journal* 13 (3): 201–32.

Zevenbergen, R. 2007. "Digital Natives Come to Preschool: Implications for Early Childhood Practice." *Contemporary Issues in Early Childhood* 8 (1): 19–29.

Touch Tablet Surprises

A Preschool Teacher's Story

by Rena Shifflet, Cheri Toledo, and Cassandra Mattoon

This article shares one teacher's experience introducing touch tablets in a preschool classroom. When used in thoughtful, deliberate ways, teachers can use tablets to promote children's cooperation, collaboration, and digital citizenship and connect technology to the real world.

Key messages

1. Teachers can use tablets to promote children's cooperation. Children can learn from each other and engage in meaningful conversations.
2. Tablets promote children's collaboration skills as children work together to create projects and complete activities using them.
3. Children develop digital citizenship as they learn how to appropriately use tablets in meaningful ways.

In your view

1. What are the three most important themes or key ideas in this article? If possible, compare your choices with those of others who have read the article.
2. How is the content of this article related to applicable early learning standards or other curriculum or program requirements?

Reflect and revisit your practice

1. What ideas in this article affirm your practice? What questions does the article raise about your teaching practices? What new approaches might you try?
2. What kinds of supports do you and other teachers need to try out these new ideas?

Let's talk

1. How do you use technology in your personal life? How does technology impact how you spend your time?
2. How does the use of technology fit into your teaching philosophy? Did the article change your view of the developmental appropriateness of using technology with young children?
3. What additional support, training, or guidance do you need to incorporate new technologies such as touch tablets into the curriculum and the classroom?

Steps you can take

1. Develop a plan for implementing a touch tablet in your program. Begin by choosing a unit you currently teach. Select a skill or concept within the unit that children's use of the tablet would reinforce. Search for an appropriate application that develops that skill or concept and plan a learning activity for children.
2. Implement your plan. Observe and document children's reactions to using the tablet. Were they motivated to learn and practice the desired skill? How easily could they manipulate the tablet and use the application?
3. Share your observations with a colleague and discuss your reflections. Determine whether you will continue incorporating technology into the curriculum and if you do, what new strategies you may try.

Glossary

App—an interactive digital game, book, information source, or creation tool that can be downloaded and used on a tablet or other mobile device.

Digital citizenship—developmentally appropriate and active uses of digital tools, media, and methods of communication and learning in safe, healthy, acceptable, responsible, and socially positive ways. Digital citizenship also means working to ensure children's equitable access to technology and interactive media experiences.

To increase your knowledge

Couse, L.J., & D.W. Chen. 2010. "A Tablet Computer for Young Children? Exploring Its Viability for Early Childhood Education." *Journal of Research on Technology in Education* 43 (1): 75–98.

Froehle, C. 2011. "10 Android Apps Perfect for Preschool-Age Kids." The Gadgeteer. http://the-gadgeteer.com/2011/07/24/10-android-apps-perfect-for-preschool-age-kids.

Furgang, K. 2011. "10 Great iPad Apps for Preschoolers." Educator.com. www.education.com/magazine/article/10-ipad-apps-preschoolers.

Yelland, N. 2005. "The Future Is Now: A Review of the Literature on the Use of Computers in Early Childhood Education (1994–2004)." *AACE Journal* 13 (3): 201–32.

Zevenbergen, R. 2007. "Digital Natives Come to Preschool: Implications for Early Childhood Practice." *Contemporary Issues in Early Childhood* 8 (1): 19–29.

Using Assistive Technology to Promote Inclusion in Early Childhood Settings

Philippa H. Campbell and M. Jeanne Wilcox

© Gordon Studer

Four-year-old Matika is learning about and practicing writing letters. Matika has cerebral palsy, a neurological disability that makes arm and hand movements—such as holding a crayon or marker—challenging. However, with the use of an iPad app, Makita only needs to move one finger across the screen to guide the lines, helping her practice writing skills with ease.

More and more, technology is becoming part of young children's lives, both at home and in early care and education programs. Technology has the same appeal for children as it does for many adults: devices are engaging and make activities enjoyable. Children with delays in development or with disabilities, such as Down syndrome, blindness, deafness, or physical limitations, may experience challenges in learning and in participating in everyday activities and routines. They may have difficulties trying to communicate or solve cognitive problems. Functional skills such as moving around the classroom, interacting

Philippa H. Campbell, PhD, is a professor of occupational therapy and director of child and family studies research programs at Thomas Jefferson University in Philadelphia, Pennsylvania. She directs research and training programs about quality services for infants, toddlers, and young children with disabilities in home, school, and community settings. Her research areas include integrated therapy, inclusion, family-centered practices, and use of adaptation and assistive technology interventions to promote children's participation.

M. Jeanne Wilcox, PhD, is a professor of speech and hearing science at Arizona State University in Tempe. She is recognized for her expertise and scholarly activity in early communication/interventions and in promoting early literacy and oral language skills in preschoolers with disabilities. She is the codirector of the Tot-N-Tech Research Institute, a collaboration between Thomas Jefferson University and Arizona State University.

naeyc® 2, 3, 9

© Ellen Senisi

with others, or using arm or hand movement during mealtime, playtime, or other ordinary activities may be difficult for children to do by themselves. While technology is engaging for most young children, for some children, technology is much more: it allows them to do things that would otherwise not be possible.

What is assistive technology?

When a child with disabilities uses a technology device to do something that she could otherwise not do, the technology device is labeled "assistive technology," or AT. While most children can communicate using words, gestures, and facial expressions, a child with communication challenges may be able to express ideas and needs only by pointing to a picture, using a voice output device, or touching a tablet with a communication application (or app). A child without mobility difficulties may be able to get around easily by walking, but a child with difficulty walking may need a walker, a gait trainer, a wheelchair, or some other device to get around without adult help.

Assistive technology is defined in many federal laws focusing on individuals with disabilities. In the Individuals with Disabilities Education Act of 2004 (IDEA), AT is defined not only as a device, but also as the services that may be needed for a child to access and use an appropriate device.

While technology is engaging for most young children, for some children, technology is much more: it allows them to do things that would otherwise not be possible.

© Ellen Senisi

Assistive technology devices

The Code of Federal Regulations (34 CFR 300.5) defines assistive technology devices as "any item, piece of equipment or product system, whether acquired commercially off the shelf, modified, or customized, that is used to increase, maintain, or improve the functional capabilities of a child with a disability" (Campbell, Milbourne, & Wilcox 2008; Sadao & Robinson 2008). For something to be considered an AT device, it must meet three criteria:

• The item, piece of equipment, or product system can be purchased off the shelf in any community store as it would for any child or may be modified or customized for an individual child.

• The purpose of using the item is to increase, maintain, or improve a child's performance of functional skills, including communication, getting around, socialization, solving problems (that is, functional use of cognitive abilities), and use of hand and arm movement in mealtime, art, or various learning center activities.

• The child using the device has a disability.

If the item does not meet all three criteria, it is not considered an AT device.

Consider the examples of 4-year-olds Sara and Matika. Sara is learning how to write letters by using an app on the iPad at the literacy center in her preschool classroom. The app has been purchased off the shelf. It helps Sara learn about and practice writing letters. Sara is learning about writing via a technology-based learning material.

Matika (introduced in the article's opening) is in the literacy center with Sara. She uses the same iPad app to learn about and practice writing letters. Matika uses the app to learn because it does not require her to hold a writing implement but only to isolate and use her finger and guide it within the lines. Just as with Sara, using the iPad helps Matika learn and practice writing. However, the difference is that Sara can learn about writing using paper and pencil or through other types of educational materials and activities, but Matika cannot, because she is unable to grasp/release objects or move her arms well. Therefore, for Sara the iPad app is not considered an AT device, but for Makita that same iPad app, used in an identical situation, is an AT device. (See "When Is Technology Considered Assistive?")

Assistive technology services

Many young children do not need special services in order to access and use AT devices effectively. However, finding appropriate devices for children with different abilities often requires skill and expertise. This is especially true for children who may need more complicated devices to successfully manage their work or participate in everyday activities, play, and routines. A child's access to an AT device may be limited because the adults in the child's life are not familiar with the range of potential devices. AT services can supplement and enhance teachers' knowledge about selecting and obtaining appropriate AT devices for children with disabilities in their classroom. An AT service is "any service that assists a child with a disability in the selection, acquisition, or use of an AT device" (34 CFR 300.6).

AT services may be provided by educators or related service providers, such as speech and language pathologists (SLP), occupational therapists (OT), or physical therapists (PT). Some school districts designate a professional from one of these disciplines to be the district's AT specialist. This specialist may provide evaluations about possible AT device use, help with functions such as obtaining the device or finding funding, and provide training/consultation for classroom teachers and children's families.

How does AT benefit children with disabilities?

Some educators may erroneously view infants and young children with disabilities as unable to fit into early care and education programs. Discrepancies between a child's skills and what is expected in a particular class-room may seem insurmountable, especially as children get older. However, careful consideration of room arrangement, environmental accommodations, furniture and equipment, schedules, activities, materials, and instructions leads to adaptations that provide opportunities for all children. Modifications that support all children may especially benefit children with disabilities by helping them be better able to learn and participate in the classroom. The three vignettes that follow are examples of such adaptations.

Sean was born with Down syndrome. As he approached his second birthday, Sean spoke words, but they were difficult to understand. Sean's mother learned from the speech and language pathologist how to make a picture communication board. She showed the board to his teachers, Donna and Eva, who made a similar one for classroom use. Sean can now express himself by talking while pointing to the pictures, and he is confident in making choices during playtime, at mealtimes, and on the playground.

Three-year-old Stephanie has frequent screaming fits, has trouble communicating, and prefers to play alone. The teacher in her early childhood program sought the help of a consultant, and together they adapted the classroom environment in several ways.

For example, they placed picture symbols everywhere, and the teacher involves all the children in using the symbols. And they made a picture schedule to hang on the wall. The children took pictures of each other in classroom activities, printed out the pictures, made photo selections, and pasted the photos onto the picture schedule. When it is time to move on to another activity, the teacher selects Stephanie to hold a special arrow and point to the picture of what the children are going to do next.

This low-tech adaptation aids all the children in making transitions, but for Stephanie, the picture schedule is a low-tech AT device that helps her understand and communicate more effectively.

Careful consideration of room arrangement, environmental accommodations, furniture and equipment, schedules, activities, materials, and instructions leads to adaptations that provide opportunities for all children.

Photo by Bonnie Blagojevic / © University of Maine Center for Community Inclusion and Disabilities Studies

Kyle's disability requires him to use AT devices to perform functional skills such as walking and talking. His kindergarten teacher has arranged the classroom with wide aisles so Kyle can operate his power chair without running into things. She obtained special equipment for Kyle, such as a device in which he can stand and chairs for sitting at a table, on the floor, and even on the toilet. The customized equipment allows Kyle to be physically included in all classroom activities. Other AT devices help him participate and learn. For example, a special spoon lets him eat independently, and a touch screen enables him to use the computer.

All of these AT devices create a bridge between what kindergartners are expected to do and what Kyle can do without assistance from others. The AT devices help him participate in the same activities as his peers, in spite of his physical disability.

Conclusion

Most devices that young children with disabilities use are either the same smartboard, tablet, or computer technology used by all children or are low-technology devices or supports that, while essential for the participation of a child with a disability, are helpful developmental supports for all children. Early childhood professionals making decisions about *all* young children's technology use, whether or not the children have disabilities, should follow the guidelines of national organizations (for example, NAEYC and the Fred Rogers Center for Early Learning and Children's Media [2012]), remembering that children with disabilities may use off-the-shelf technology devices differently from children without disabilities. For example, children may use tablets to play games, draw, or learn about concepts such as shape and color. Children with

Early childhood professionals making decisions about *all* young children's technology use, whether or not the children have disabilities, should follow the guidelines of national organizations

40

Spotlight on Young Children and Technology

disabilities may interact with tablets for the same purposes, but they may also use special apps that make the tablets communication devices. The amount of time recommended for children to interact with screen devices is not a consideration when they are used by children with disabilities for functional purposes such as communication. In those instances, the devices are AT and need to be available for children all day long.

In the end, the important thing to remember for children with disabilities is a point that has been made many times about using technology with any child—it is not about the device but about how the device is integrated into early childhood programs to appropriately support children's development, learning, and participation.

References

Campbell, P.H., S. Milbourne, & M. J. Wilcox. 2008. "Adaptation Interventions to Promote Participation in Natural Settings." *Infants and Young Children* 21 (2): 94–106.

Individuals with Disabilities Education Improvement Act (IDEA) of 2004. P.L. 108-446.

NAEYC & Fred Rogers Center for Early Learning and Children's Media at Saint Vincent College. 2012. "Technology and Interactive Media as Tools in Early Childhood Programs Serving Children from Birth through Age 8." Joint position statement. Washington, DC: NAEYC. www.naeyc.org/files/naeyc/file/positions/PS_technology_WEB2.pdf.

Sadao, K.C., & N. Robinson. 2010. *Assistive Technology for Young Children: Creating Inclusive Learning Environments.* Baltimore, MD: Brookes.

Photo by Bonnie Blagojevic / © University of Maine Center for Community Inclusion and Disabilities Studies

The 5 Ws of Inclusion

Leah Schoenberg Muccio

What is inclusion?

Inclusion is a philosophy and practice that supports the rights of all children, regardless of their abilities, to participate actively in everyday activities within their communities (Osgood 2005).

What is early childhood inclusion?

Inclusion in early education settings encompasses coordinated and specialized services, as well as individualized accommodations, that enable children with disabilities to participate fully in play and learning experiences. All children should experience a sense of belonging in these settings. The joint position statement from the Division for Early Childhood (DEC) and NAEYC (2009) provides a formal definition of early childhood inclusion. It describes the goals of inclusion for children with and without disabilities as a sense of belonging, positive social relationships and friendships, and development and learning to reach their full potential.

Who participates in inclusion?

Many infants, toddlers, preschoolers, and school-age children with disabilities play and learn with their peers who do not have disabilities in inclusive early childhood settings. Children may come to the early childhood setting with a disability diagnosis or become eligible for special education services while in the program. For inclusion to be successful, classroom teachers, special education teachers, related service providers, administrators, and families must collaborate to ensure children with disabilities have full access to the play and learning experiences in the classroom, participate as active members of the classroom community, and receive the appropriate supports to be fully included.

Where does the support for inclusion come from?

The inclusion of children with disabilities in general education settings is supported by (1) federal regulations, especially the Individuals with Disabilities Education Act (IDEA), which requires that all children be educated in the least restrictive environment; (2) increasing societal acceptance of ability diversity, reflecting the value of providing opportunities for every child; and (3) research affirming the benefits of inclusive settings for children with and without disabilities (e.g., Hundert et al. 1998; Rafferty, Piscitelli, & Boettcher 2003; Kalambouka et al. 2007).

Why inclusion?

Children with disabilities have increased opportunities for learning from peers, for social interactions and relationships and for achievement of their individual goals. Children without disabilities benefit from increased opportunities to respect and appreciate diversity, form meaningful friendships, and have access to increased resources, such as more time working with teachers in small groups. Children with and without disabilities do better academically and socially in inclusive settings (Baker, Wang, & Walberg 1994). Inclusion is beneficial for children with and without disabilities and can be a wonderfully rewarding experience for children, families, and teachers.

To read the entire DEC/NAEYC position statement, go to www.naeyc.org/files/naeyc/file/positions/DEC_NAEYC_EC_updatedKS.pdf.

References

Baker, E.T., M.C. Wang, & H.J. Walberg. 1994. "The Effects of Inclusion on Learning." *Educational Leadership* 52 (4): 33–35.

Division for Early Childhood & NAEYC. 2009. "Early Childhood Inclusion." Joint position statement. Chapel Hill, NC: FPG Child Development Institute. www.naeyc.org/files/naeyc/file/positions/DEC_NAEYC_EC_updatedKS.pdf.

Hundert, J., B. Mahoney, F. Mundy, & M.L. Vernon. 1998. "A Descriptive Analysis of Developmental and Social Gains of Children with Severe Disabilities in Segregated and Inclusive Preschools in Southern Ontario." *Early Childhood Research Quarterly* 13 (1): 49–65. doi:10.1016/S0885-2006(99)80025-8.

Kalambouka, A., P. Farrell, A. Dyson, & I. Kaplan. 2007. "The Impact of Placing Pupils with Special Education Needs in Mainstream Schools on the Achievement of Their Peers." *Educational Research* 49 (4): 365–82. doi:10.1080/00131880701717222.

Osgood, R.L. 2005. *The History of Inclusion in the United States.* Washington, DC: Gallaudet University Press.

Rafferty, Y., V. Piscitelli, & C. Boettcher. 2003. "The Impact of Inclusion on Language Development and Social Competence among Preschoolers with Disabilities." *Exceptional Children* 69 (4): 467–79. www.cec.sped.org/Content/NavigationMenu/AboutCEC/International/StepbyStep/ResourceCenter/InclusiveEducation General/VOLUME69NUMBER4Summer2003_EC_Article-5.pdf.

Leah Schoenberg Muccio, PhD, is an editorial associate at NAEYC.

Using Assistive Technology to Promote Inclusion in Early Childhood Settings

by Philippa H. Campbell and M. Jeanne Wilcox

This article defines assistive technology (AT) devices and services, explores how teachers may effectively and appropriately integrate them into their early childhood programs, and describes the benefits of using such devices and services. It provides resources and examples of ways that teachers address the individual needs of children with disabilities.

Key messages

1. Assistive technology devices enable children with disabilities to do things they could not otherwise do and to be included more fully in play and learning experiences.
2. Many low- and high-tech devices used by all children may be adapted for use by children with disabilities.
3. Teachers must plan carefully how they will integrate an assistive technology device into the classroom to best address a child's individual needs.

In your view

1. What are the three most important themes or key ideas in this article? If possible, compare your choices with those of others who have read the article.
2. How is the content of this article related to applicable early learning standards or other curriculum or program requirements?

Reflect and revisit your practice

1. What ideas in this article affirm your practice? What questions does the article raise about your teaching practices? What new approaches might you try?
2. What kinds of assistance do you and other teachers need to try out these new ideas?

Let's talk

1. Think about the children in your program. How does the article's content relate to what you know already about meeting the needs of individual children, especially those with disabilities?
2. If children in your setting already use assistive technology devices, how have the devices influenced the children's learning experiences? Which devices work well? What challenges have you encountered?
3. How has the information in this article changed the way you think about using assistive technology devices to promote inclusion in the classroom? Which new strategies do you plan to try?

Steps you can take

1. Select a child in your classroom who would benefit from using an assistive technology device to address his or her individual needs. Develop a plan to obtain the assistive technology device and to introduce it and use it with the child.
2. Implement the plan, and document the child's experiences using the assistive technology device. How did the use of assistive technology affect the child's opportunities to participate in all program activities and routines? What were the benefits and challenges of using the device—for the child and for you?
3. Reflect on your new practices. What changes would you make integrating an assistive technology device into your setting next time? What other devices would you like to use?

Glossary

Adaptations—a range of strategies to promote a child's access to learning opportunities, from making simple changes to the environment and materials to obtaining and helping a child use special equipment.

Assistive technology device—any item, piece of equipment, or product that is used to increase, maintain, or improve the functional capabilities of a child with a disability.

Functional skills—skills used every day in different environments. They include communicating, moving around, socializing, and solving problems.

To increase your knowledge

Division for Early Childhood & NAEYC. 2009. "Early Childhood Inclusion." A joint position statement of the Division for Early Childhood and NAEYC. Chapel Hill, NC: FPG Child Development Institute. www.naeyc.org/positionstatements.

The National Early Childhood Technical Assistance Center (NECTAC). "Assistive Technology Overview." www.nectac.org/topics/atech/overview.asp.

Sadao, K.C., & N. Robinson. 2010. *Assistive Technology for Young Children: Creating Inclusive Learning Environments.* Baltimore, MD: Brookes.

Tots-N-Tech (TNT). Help Desk. http://tnt.asu.edu/tnt-helpdesk.

Exploring Elephant Seals in New Jersey

Preschoolers Use Collaborative Multimedia Albums

Victoria B. Fantozzi

© Gordon Studer

Victoria B. Fantozzi, PhD, is an assistant professor of elementary and childhood education at William Paterson University in Wayne, New Jersey. She teaches education courses in emergent literacy, and observes and researches at the Child Development Center.

The author thanks Cindy Gennarelli, Elizabeth Morgado, Denielle Carr, Jennifer Hacker, and Janirys Lebron, the wonderful teachers in this classroom, who use all tools at their disposal to inspire curiosity and a love of learning in all children.

Photos by Bonnie Blagojevic / © University of Maine Center for Community Inclusion and Disability Studies.

naeyc® 2, 3

Three children sit excitedly around the computer. Their teacher, Miss Janirys, says, "I wonder what Miss Liz and Miss Cindy have for us today." Miss Cindy and Miss Liz are at a conference in California. She clicks to a picture of an elephant seal sleeping on the sand. Next to it is an avatar photo of Miss Liz. Miss Janirys clicks on a photo of Miss Liz, and the children listen to what she posted for them earlier in the day. Miss Liz says, "This is an elephant seal. Elephant seals don't have any ears, and an elephant seal is so big it could never fit in your mommy's or daddy's car." Miss Janirys turns to the children. "Who would like to tell Miss Liz something?" They all bounce at the chance.

Miss Janirys helps Juanita write, "What do elephant seals eat?" Tommy asks to speak into the microphone. He says, "An elephant seal won't fit into your grandma's or grandpa's or Aunt Bonnie's or Angelo's car." It's Shea's turn next. She says, "Why does an elephant seal have no ears? How can it hear with no ears? Because I can hear when I have ears."

The children scamper off to the other centers, knowing they can check back for their responses from Miss Liz and Miss Cindy all the way across the country. They are excited to hear what their teachers have to say. Later in the day, they get their answers. Miss Liz answers Juanita's question about what elephant seals eat and reaffirms that elephant seals would not fit in anyone's car. She adds, "Elephant seals would even weigh more than the car." Miss Cindy adds, "The elephant seals do not have ears; you are absolutely right. What they have are little holes on either side of their head, and the little holes are just like ears that allow them to hear. Great question. I like the way you are thinking!"

opportunities to engage with technologies in developmentally appropriate ways. Given appropriate experiences, young children can develop technology-handling skills in the same way they learn to handle or interact with books and environmental print (NAEYC & Fred Rogers Center 2012). It is important that early childhood educators are prepared with tools for teaching children to think critically about the information that they have at their fingertips. These tools are not just toys to satisfy the new interests of the digital natives, but can be used to heighten interest and motivation (Bers, New, & Boudreau 2004).

This article shares the experiences of one multiage (3- to 5-year-olds) preschool classroom's use of VoiceThread. The purpose of the article is to introduce early childhood educators to technology that allows children to interact with media in ways that align with the joint position statement "Technology and Interactive Media as Tools in Early Childhood Programs Serving Children from Birth through Age 8," from NAEYC and the Fred Rogers Center (2012). NAEYC and the Fred Rogers Center promote the use of technology that is engaging and empowering, and allows children to extend their experiences in ways that promote cognitive and social development. VoiceThread is a form of web-based social media that enables users to create slideshows that can hold documents, images, and/or videos. A user (either a child or a teacher, depending on the project) can give access to others, and they may comment (either in audio, text, or video) on any part of the thread. This tool offers multiple pathways for children to communicate and collaborate with others. The children in this class could choose to speak, type, or dictate their comments. This variety of communication methods supports prosocial communicative behaviors as well as emergent literacy skills.

Emerging technologies, from new social media to podcasts, are changing the definition of what it means to be literate in our society. Children will be expected to be

This is an example of one way VoiceThread—a website that allows users to create multimedia slideshows, or "threads," and then open these threads to other users for commentary or collaboration—is used in a Reggio Emilia-inspired suburban preschool classroom. These preschoolers are experts at observing and sharing their questions because of the environment their teachers have created. Their observations do not have to stop because they are in New Jersey and two of their teachers are on the West Coast. Miss Liz and Miss Cindy use VoiceThread to introduce them to new concepts and animals they have never seen, spark their curiosity, and connect them to the world outside their classroom.

VoiceThread in the preschool classroom

As a new generation of children enters preschool, early childhood educators will find "digital natives" in their classrooms—children growing up with technology so fully integrated into their lives that they may approach and process new material differently than previous generations (Prensky 2001a, 2001b; Oblinger & Oblinger 2005; Zevenbergen & Logan 2008). Certainly, access to technology is not equal. Educators will find children who have grown up with access to interactive media and touch screens, but they will also find children who have never had access to these resources.

In preschool settings, it is the early childhood educator's responsibility to ensure that children receive

Miss Liz and Miss Cindy use VoiceThread to introduce the children to new concepts and animals they have never seen, spark their curiosity, and connect them to the world outside their classroom.

mutiliterate; that is, to be comfortable with print media as well as the changing, collaborative, and visual media available through the Internet (New London Group 1996; Heintz et al. 2010). As a result, Borsheim, Merrit, and Reed (2008) state that it is important for

> teachers who employ a multiliteracies' pedagogy [to] offer their students ample opportunities to access, evaluate, search, sort, gather, and read information from a variety of multimedia and multimodal sources and invite students to collaborate in real and virtual spaces to produce and publish multimedia and multimodal texts for a variety of audiences and purposes. (87)

Multimodal sources use more than words to communicate to the reader or viewer. Examples of these sources, such as interactive web pages, use a combination of avenues to communicate (for example, text and video). Because multimodal texts are increasing in availability and prevalence, it is important that we teach children how to interact with these texts. The multimodal combination of text, images, and voices incorporated in the VoiceThread tool helps children become multiliterate.

In addition, the multimedia options allow children to approach what they see and hear from an inquiry stance. The children in this class talk about what they notice in the pictures and ask questions of their teacher and their peers. This feature helps teachers in this classroom emphasize ways that interweaving of children's and teachers' voices contributes to learning (Juzwik et al. 2008).

In order to allow family participation, the teachers created a secure community in which they could control who was able to access and comment on the class threads. (Teachers grant access by adding a family's e-mail address to a list in their privacy setting.) Teachers granted access to all families so they could view and discuss the VoiceThreads at home with their children, and,

The multimodal combination of text, images, and voices incorporated in the VoiceThread tool helps children become multiliterate.

if they chose, add their own comments. VoiceThread has many free options on the website (see "What Is the Cost?"), so once invited the families could access it from any home or public computer.

Classrooms whose families do not have easy access to a computer may consider hosting VoiceThread Nights at which the students present their work or at which a computer lab is open so that families can read and comment on a class thread together. Empowering families to engage in thoughtful use of a secure website helps them become advocates for appropriate uses of technology for their children.

Extending *beyond* the four walls

Web-based technology allows children to connect to peers, professionals, and in this case their teachers, in ways they could not before. The children in this New Jersey classroom would not likely have seen an elephant seal in person or have been able to participate in the Chinese New Year parade in San Francisco (while in California, Miss Liz and Miss Cindy also posted pictures of the Chinese dragons dancing in the parade), but this technology allowed them to not only view pictures, but engage in a conversation with their teachers and their peers about the images. The children in the class became connected to places they could not access before.

The previous year, these teachers used the VoiceThread tool to connect closer to home—to another New Jersey preschool classroom. The classes participated in a unit on robots. Each class explored robots in books and built their own robot using the same materials. They shared pictures and their separate processes through VoiceThread. Miss Liz reported that using VoiceThread to see the other class's robot influenced the conversation in the classroom. She said, "The conversation emerged: How are the robots the same? How are they different? Do you think these robots would like each other if they met? There was a lot of language developing from the conversation, and they were able to listen to the other children talk about their robot." Interacting with another class doing the same project encouraged the children to engage in higher order thinking. They examined how the same project could be interpreted differently by another class and also thought more about the choices they had

What Is the Cost?

VoiceThread offers a free account specifically for educators called the VTeducator. This account offers unlimited viewing and listening, as well as text or audio commenting. This option does have limits on phone commenting, the number of VoiceThreads (50 at a time with up to 50 slides each), and webcam commenting (the site owners say they have yet to see a free account holder exceed the webcam limit). There are also upgrades for classroom or schoolwide accounts that allow each child to create an individual account and allow the teacher to manage and edit children's postings. The school subscription cost varies depending on the number of classrooms. All of the examples shared in this article were accomplished with a free account.

made. Although Miss Liz noted that at first the children were a little shy about talking to children they had not met, after the first few exchanges they lost their shyness and VoiceThread became just another tool at their disposal. Often, after building a new robot part or after having a class discussion, the children would say, "Hey, why don't we send this to the other class?" Miss Liz's preschoolers became comfortable with this multiliterate way of reporting and receiving ideas through photo, text, and audio exchanges.

Because of these positive experiences, Miss Liz and Miss Cindy decided to use VoiceThread for communicating with the children while they were in California. As experienced educators, they had used a variety of technologies (as well as other nontechnological resources) in the past to extend the children's learning outside the four walls of the classroom. The previous year, Miss Liz had traveled to Mexico to learn more about the migration of the monarch butterfly (the development and migration of which the children study every year). While in Mexico she used a blog to communicate with the children. She posted daily, and the children had opportunities at home and at school to comment. Although she interacted with the children through these blog postings, she felt that something was missing. Miss Cindy had been introduced to VoiceThread through a conference, and suggested that she and Miss Liz try it. They found the website easy to use; they did not need any specific training, rather they just "played around," exploring the website, tutorials, and experimenting with the different posting options.

Miss Liz found that for the children interacting with VoiceThread, there was a different quality to the experience. The option to dictate, type, or audio record the message allowed the children to connect in a more engaging and exciting way.

Miss Liz found that for the children interacting with VoiceThread, there was a different quality to the experience. The option to dictate, type, or audio record the message allowed the children to connect in a more engaging and exciting way. The children loved to hear their teachers' voices, and most enjoyed hearing their own voices as well. This year, continuing their study of monarch butterflies, the teachers posted a picture of a cluster of butterflies, using VoiceThread, and encouraged the children to estimate how many butterflies had clustered on the tree. The children conferred and posted their estimates. When their teachers returned to New Jersey, the children excitedly asked, "Did you count all the butterflies?" Miss Liz said, "The children weren't there physically, but they were there through VoiceThread. They could be a part of the experience."

Extending *within* the four walls

In a world in which children are increasingly bombarded with media, NAEYC cautions against overuse or overexposure to technology in the classroom (2012). I was drawn to write about this tool because of its ability to spark children's interest and extend classroom discussions and play. The children were very interested and engaged by what they heard, saw, and commented on in the VoiceThread. Even before Miss Liz and Miss Cindy

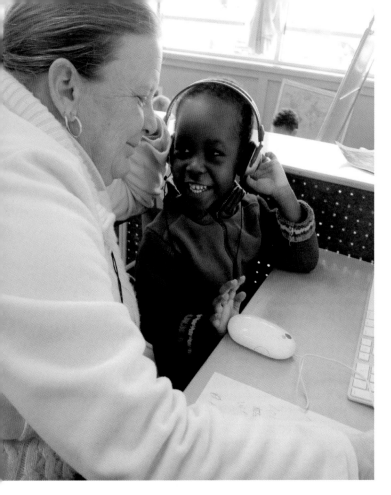

flies. The children connected to the idea of "California" and travel because they had been able to experience it through the audio and pictures their teachers posted. This medium allowed them to form a concept they explored in their play.

When Miss Liz and Miss Cindy returned, the children were eager to talk to their teachers about their trip because in a way they had gone on this trip with them. Miss Liz found that her discussions with the children were much richer than when she had returned from previous trips. She recounts a discussion they had about the elephant seal upon her return.

Julie: Remember, you were tiptoeing to the elephant seal? Is this *(with hand)* how big it is?

Miss Liz: No, it is much bigger!

Julie: Well, how much bigger?

Adunni: Let's measure with ourselves! We lie down and you tell us when to stop. (*The children lie down and use their bodies to estimate the elephant seal's size.*)

Interacting through VoiceThread kindled the children's interest in something they were not able to experience firsthand. Supported by their teachers, the children transferred what they learned through their interactions with the media and teachers on VoiceThread to their interactions in school, enriching their class discussions and play.

Beyond this classroom

These teachers used VoiceThread to engage children in inquiry and connect them to places outside the classroom, but certainly there are other ways of using it in the classroom. In fact, teachers have become the early adopters of this technology, so much so that VoiceThread expanded its site to include Ed.VoiceThread.com, specifically for educators. Ed.VoiceThread offers the same collaboration and communication options, but also includes options for children to open class accounts without an e-mail address and allows the teacher the ability to manage and monitor these accounts. The following are suggestions for using the tool throughout the early childhood years.

A tool for collaboration. Children can use Voice-Thread to collaborate within the classroom and with other classes within their school, or with classes in other schools. Children can video record or photograph science experiments they are conducting, and then share and compare the results with other classes. They can post photos or stories from the headlines and engage children in other parts of the country or the world in conversation about an issue important to them.

A new kind of report. Teachers and students can use this tool to explore alternate ways of presenting information. Rather than writing a science report or book

returned, they asked their other teachers, who were still in New Jersey, to help them research elephant seals on the Internet. As multiliterate learners the children also extended this experience into the nontechnological world of their discussions and play. Quon explored elephant seals through art—he made his own clay sculpture of an elephant seal. Similarly, the children incorporated their knowledge of the trip into their play. During the class's study of monarch butterflies, Miss Janirys read a book about monarch butterflies' migration to California. The children connected the butterflies' trip to the trip they knew their teachers were on in the same state.

Miss Janirys: This is a map. The butterfly will fly across the country to California, but it starts on this side of the country. We live here. Does anyone know what state we live in?

Satish: New Jersey! Miss Cindy and Miss Liz flew to California! We could go too!

Madeline: We could play in the block center.

Gia: We could go to California and to Mexico, two places!

Quon: I will be a passenger!

Satish: I will drive.

After the story in small-group time, the children enacted their vision in the block center, creating an airplane, complete with tickets for each child and a pilot to fly them to see Miss Cindy, Miss Liz, and the butter-

Preparing children to become multiliterate consumers of media means teachers need to help children understand how to navigate between and across multiple forms of media.

review, they can construct VoiceThreads that share what they learned in a multimodal way. Children can create a presentation on any topic, using photos, documents, and videos to communicate ideas and receive feedback from their teachers and peers.

A professional development tool. Teachers can use this tool to communicate with other teachers. Not only can they invite colleagues to view and interact with the VoiceThreads that were successful in their classroom, but they can create a VoiceThread to serve as a forum to share other teaching tools and goals. Teachers can post documents from lessons for comments, find help with video or audio recording problems, or share student work for feedback.

A different kind of show-and-tell. Children can virtually share something of their own. They can upload pictures or videos of their toys, family members, or pets, and then narrate or type what they would like the class to know. Children can share family gatherings, traditions, or even family vacations. This activity can continue throughout the year—even over school breaks. The class's and teacher's comments and questions can keep learning going and create, or continue, a sense of community in the classroom.

Final thoughts

The teachers in this classroom see the children as competent, capable, and independent learners. It is this view of children, not the technology, that empowers the children to ask questions and explore their world. It is important for teachers to use their professional judgment as to how, when, and if they use VoiceThread in their classrooms. However, preparing children to become multiliterate consumers of media means teachers need to help children understand how to navigate between and across multiple forms of media, as well as help them think about when and why they might draw on specific technologies to achieve specific purposes. VoiceThread is one tool among many (see "Beyond VoiceThread" on page 50) that helps teachers achieve these goals.

In addition, educators must always consider the well-being of children. VoiceThread offers both public and private options for sharing the threads teachers and children create. This class chose to have their VoiceThreads viewed only by those they invited. Others in the Voice-Thread community may choose to share their threads publicly. Educators need to carefully consider these options and the best interests of the children, while keeping the children's families in mind. Once they have made careful decisions, teachers and children can connect, communicate, and explore the world around them with the help of VoiceThread.

References

Bers, M.U., R.S. New, & L. Boudreau. 2004. "Teaching and Learning When No One Is Expert: Children and Parents Explore Technology." *Early Childhood Research and Practice* 6 (2). http://ecrp.uiuc.edu/v6n2/bers.html.

Borsheim, C., K. Merritt, & D. Reed. 2008. "Beyond Technology for Technology's Sake: Advancing Multiliteracies in the Twenty-First Century." *The Clearing House: A Journal of Educational Strategies, Issues and Ideas* 82 (2): 87–90.

Heintz, A., C. Borsheim, S. Caughlan, M.M. Juzwik, & M. Sherry. 2010. "Video-based Response and Revision: Dialogic Instruction Using Video and Web 2.0 Technologies." *Contemporary Issues in Technology and Teacher Education* 10 (2): 175–96. www.citejournal.org/vol10/iss2/languagearts/article2.cfm.

Juzwik, M.M., M. Nystrand, S. Kelly & M.B. Sherry. 2008. "Oral Narrative Genres as Dialogic Resources for Classroom Literature Study: A Contextualized Case Study of Conversational Narrative Discussion." *American Educational Research Journal* 45 (4): 1111–54.

NAEYC & Fred Rogers Center for Early Learning and Children's Media at Saint Vincent College. 2012. "Technology and Interactive Media as Tools in Early Childhood Programs Serving Children from Birth through Age 8." Joint position statement. Washington, DC: NAEYC. www.naeyc.org/files/naeyc/file/positions/PS_technology_WEB2.pdf.

New London Group. 1996. "A Pedagogy of Multiliteracies: Designing Social Futures." *Harvard Educational Review* 66 (1): 60–92.

Oblinger, D.G., & J.L. Oblinger. 2005. "Is it Age or IT? First Steps toward Understanding the Net Generation." In *Educating the Net Generation*, eds. Oblinger & Oblinger, 2.1–2.20. Boulder, CO: EDUCAUSE.

Prensky, M. 2001a. "Digital Natives, Digital Immigrants. Part 1." *On the Horizon* 9 (5): 1–6. www.marcprensky.com/writing/Prensky%20-%20.Digital%20Natives,%20Digital%20Immigrants%20-%20Part1.pdf.

Prensky, M. 2001b. "Digital Natives, Digital Immigrants: Do They Really Think Differently? Part 2." *On the Horizon* 9 (6): 1–6. www.marcprensky.com/writing/prensky%20-%20digital%20natives,%20digital%20immigrants%20-%20part2.pdf.

Zevenbergen, R., & H. Logan. 2008. "Computer Use by Preschool Children: Rethinking Practice as Digital Natives Come to Preschool." *Australian Journal of Early Childhood* 33 (1): 37–44.

Resources for teachers

Examples of VoiceThreads

Ed.VoiceThread digital library. A digital library containing examples of successful teacher-created VoiceThread projects from kindergarten to college level. Each entry includes a brief description of the assignment, its goals, possible challenges, and tips for successful completion. The database is maintained by the creators of VoiceThread; they encourage educators to submit successful VoiceThread projects, and then select exemplary submissions to include in the library. **http://ed.voicethread.com/about/library**

VoiceThread 4 Education wiki. This wiki (a website that allows users to post and edit content) contains teacher-created VoiceThread projects for grades K–12 and VoiceThreads used for professional development, as well as resources and tips for the best use of the tool. **http://voicethread4education.wikispaces.com**

Technical guides

"Getting Started in the Classroom." A guide specifically for educators. **http://ed.voicethread.com/media/misc/getting_started_in_the_classroom.pdf**

Basic support and FAQs. This section of the VoiceThread site offers answers to questions frequently asked about setting up a new account or new thread. **http://voicethread.com/support/howto/Basics**

"VoiceThread: A Tool for Having Conversations around Media." Basic setup instructions and tips for teachers using the tools from VoiceThread.com. **www.wpunj.edu/dotAsset/236980.pdf**

"Using VoiceThread for Digital Conversations." Tips and guidelines for creating successful VoiceThreads. **http://digitallyspeaking.pbworks.com/w/page/17791585/VoicethreadiceThreads**

"An Educator's Guide to VoiceThread." Although aimed at educators of older children, this PDF contains a basic introduction and screenshots to guide a novice through the site. **http://voicethread.com/media/misc/getting_started_educator_mpb.pdf**

Beyond VoiceThread

Many other forms of social media allow children and teachers to collaborate over the Internet. These websites allow users to post media for discussion and are popular among teachers.

Glogster is a website that allows users to create interactive multimedia posters. Users create their own wall of media including backgrounds, text, audio, and video. Much like VoiceThread, this site offers packages for school use. http://Edu.glogster.com

Vialogues is a free collaborative site from EdLab. It is designed to create discussions around video. Users can upload video and invite others to an online discussion. Much the same as VoiceThreads, a Vialogue can be made private, allowing only invitees to view and comment on the chosen video. Although mainly used by secondary and college-level students, early childhood educators can encourage critical multiliteracy through discussions about videos and media advertisements. https://vialogues.com

Facebook is a popular medium with which many are familiar. It can be used as an educational tool as well as a social tool. Although Facebook's security does not allow children younger than 13 to independently use it, teachers can create profiles to share with children. Teachers can post content such as images, video, or links to other web pages. www.facebook.com

Exploring Elephant Seals in New Jersey

by Victoria B. Fantozzi

Preschoolers Use Collaborative Multimedia Albums

This article shares ways teachers can use collaborative multimedia albums—presentations using video clips, voice recordings, and images—that allow children to explore new topics, document their work, and communicate with other children in early childhood settings.

Key messages

1. Collaborative multimedia albums allow children to explore places and topics (such as elephant seals) that they might not have access to otherwise.
2. Collaborative technology gives children the opportunity to communicate in multimodal ways (through audio, video, pictures, text, and more), which supports their multiliteracy.
3. Children using these technologies go beyond the computer and incorporate what they learn into their play and their conversations with friends and teachers.

In your view

1. What are the three most important themes or key ideas in this article? If possible, compare your choices with those of others who have read the article.
2. How is the content of this article related to applicable early learning standards or other curriculum or program requirements?

Reflect and revisit your practice

1. What ideas in this article affirm your practice? What questions does the article raise about your teaching practices? What new approaches might you try?
2. What kinds of supports do you and other teachers need to try out these new ideas?

Let's talk

1. In what ways do you currently support children's multiliteracy? How might multimedia technology enhance children's learning experiences?
2. What resources or support would you need to incorporate collaborative multimedia albums in your setting?

Steps you can take

1. Develop a plan to use a collaborative multimedia technology (such as VoiceThread or Glogster) with the children in your setting. Determine your purpose for using the technology (to document a project, tell an electronic story, communicate with another class, share children's experiences, or others). Experiment with the technology on your own. Plan how you will introduce the project to the children (small groups may work best).
2. Implement the project and observe and document children's experiences. In what ways do children extend their learning into play while away from the computer? Or in conversations with friends and family? How does their work reflect or extend the content you are teaching?
3. Share the children's experiences using the technology with families either electronically or during a special multimedia presentation night. Answer any questions and address concerns families share with you.

Glossary

Multimodal—refers to multiple ways of knowing or communicating; this could be through sound, text, images, movement, or combinations of these.

Multiliteracy—abilities that go beyond traditional literacy skills (such as communicating, reading, fluency, vocabulary, writing, and word study) to more complex ones, such as understandings of media and digital technologies, and the ability to critically process information.

To increase your knowledge

"7 Things You Should Know about VoiceThread." 2009. Educause Learning Initiative. http://net.educause.edu/ir/library/pdf/ELI7050.pdf.

Berson, I.R., & M.J. Berson, eds. 2010. High-Tech Tots: Childhood in a Digital World. Charlotte, NC: Information Age Publishing.

Brand, S., & S. Byrd. 2011. "Using VoiceThread to Promote Learning Engagement and Success for All Students." *Teaching Exceptional Children* 43 (4): 28–37.

Gillis, A., K. Luthin, H. Parette, & C. Blum. 2012. "Using VoiceThread to Create Meaningful Receptive and Expressive Learning Activities for Young Children." *Early Childhood Education Journal* 40 (3): 1-9. DOI 10.1007/s10643-012-0521-1.

Mitchell, S. 2009. "Ten Tips for Involving Families through Internet Communication." *Young Children* 64 (5): 46–49.

iDocument

How Smartphones and Tablets Are Changing Documentation in Preschool and Primary Classrooms

Will Parnell and Jackie Bartlett

© Gordon Studer

Will Parnell, EdD, is assistant professor in curriculum and instruction and early childhood education at Portland State University (PSU). He is pedagogical director of PSU's Helen Gordon Child Development Center and has authored publications about children's and teachers' Reggio-inspired experiences in the center. Will coordinates the master's specialization in early childhood education for the Graduate School of Education's Curriculum and Instruction Department.

Jackie Bartlett, MS, is the director of Portland Baby School. She currently teaches kindergarten in Portland, Oregon. Her education interests include the effects of mobile technology on documentation practices.

Photos courtesy of the authors.

 **2, 3**

Zoe builds a tower in the block area, taking care to leave a hole at the top. Her teacher pulls a smartphone from her pocket and snaps a picture. "What are you building, Zoe?" she asks. "Rapunzel's tower," Zoe replies. The children have been studying the story of Rapunzel for the last two weeks.

"This is Rapunzel," says Aster, showing the teacher a cutout drawing of a person. A piece of ribbon is taped to the head. "I see that she has very long hair," the teacher says, snapping another picture. "Will Rapunzel's hair reach the ground from the window of the tower?" The children see that the hair is too short to reach the bottom of Zoe's tower, and they gather materials from the cut-and-color table to fix it.

By sliding her thumb across the screen of the smartphone, the teacher is ready to record video as the preschoolers explore measurement and spatial relationships while building their fine motor skills. Two minutes later, she presses an arrow icon and uploads the video to her classroom's password-protected video-sharing account. After school, she creates a blog entry about the latest math exploration to emerge from the Rapunzel study and adds photos to the text. The teacher does all of this in a few minutes, using a blog-writing application on her smartphone. This Reggio-inspired early childhood teacher has her finger on the pulse of the latest technology for "making learning visible" (Project Zero & Reggio Children 2001)—that is, documenting young children's learning to better understand and shape it (Rinaldi 2006).

At home, parents ask their children about their day at school while viewing the classroom blog. Because of the blog documentation, parents can ask specific questions about the activities. The questions give the children an opportunity to share their learning and to think deeply

Teachers can use smart-phones and tablets every day to take photos, record video and audio, and make notes, then integrate them into daily blogs and online portfolios that parents can access.

about their experiences. For example, after Zoe's dad reviews the video of the children remaking Rapunzel's hair, he asks her questions such as, "How did you know when Rapunzel's hair was long enough to reach the ground?"

With the increased prevalence of smartphones, laptops, tablet computers, and other digital technologies, knowledge about and familiarity with the educational uses for these devices is important for early childhood teachers documenting children's learning. A single device can manage many functions that previously required a number of steps for inclusion on a website or blog. As teachers' technology skills increase, organizing and reproducing facets of children's learning experiences becomes easy.

Teachers can use smartphones every day to take photos, record video and audio, and make notes, then integrate them into daily blogs and online portfolios that parents can access. They can do all of this as the events of the day unfold, saving valuable planning time and giving families a window into their children's learning at school. As an integral part of teaching, this digital documentation process—gathering and reproducing trails and traces of children's learning experiences—is a topic worthy of study. Technology can be a powerful tool for strengthening children's home-school connection (NAEYC & Fred Rogers Center 2012).

We two authors, Jackie Bartlett and Will Parnell, teacher researchers at a Portland, Oregon, preschool and primary school respectively, joined together to investigate the question of what digital and

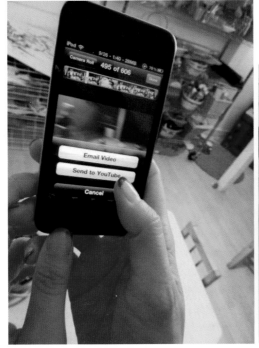

technological documentation processes look like in teachers' everyday practices. We hope our collaboration sheds light on the value of technology in documenting children's learning.

Why documentation matters

Documentation has many important defining characteristics. It is the process of observing and recording children's development and learning. As part of the process, teachers ask questions, collect data on the children (work artifacts, quotations, photos, audio recordings, and such), interpret the data, and develop an ongoing dialogue about the process with colleagues, parents, and the children themselves. This helps everyone understand the children's development and learning and how to promote it.

Interpreting children's learning

Although documentation is a record of the events that occur in children's school experiences, making learning visible is not objective. Rinaldi (2006) illustrates this point in her description of the act of photographing a child. She suggests that when we take a photograph of a child, we construct, rather than capture, reality: we do not photograph the child, we photograph our idea of the child. Documentation, therefore, is not a standardized measurement of a child's achievement; it is the teacher's subjective and participatory assessment—her interpretation—of the child or group of children's work and thinking.

When we have a record of a child's learning, we have a tool for interpretation as well as a tool for reporting and understanding learning—sometimes in surprising and new ways. Malaguzzi identifies interpretation as a critical part of

the documentation process (1998). He acknowledges the power that interpretation has in shaping curriculum and understanding the nature of learning: "To find clarity and dispel the fog [in the recorded texts of children] yields a great deal of information about the thoughts of children. Through careful interpretation, one learns that children continually attempt to draw connections among things and thereby grow and learn" (95). Malaguzzi's clarity concept lends itself to images of children as strong, competent, and capable learners that challenge assumptions about what children can achieve: "Those who have the image of the child as fragile, incomplete, weak, made of glass, gain something from this belief only for themselves. We don't need that as an image of children" (Malaguzzi 1994). By believing that children are competent, teachers promote their competence. Through documentation, teachers glean information that helps direct learning and bridge the gap between what children have learned and what they learn next.

Shaping children's self-perceptions

Documenting children's learning affects their self-images in positive ways. By committing time and energy to documenting a child's work, teachers affirm that the child is a valued member of the learning community. Rinaldi (2006) states that the child exists when others recognize that what he says is important. Documentation is an expression of this recognition. Scheinfeld, Haigh, and Scheinfeld find that there is a substantial, affective benefit of careful listening and documentation: "The children experience that their expressions of interests, motives, emotions, ideas, and capabilities are noted and embraced by the teacher and are causes of the teacher's responses to them. Thus, the children experience themselves as fully existing, valid, worthwhile, and cherished in the mind and heart of the teacher" (2008, 17).

Further, by presenting the children's work and documentation to the children as part of the learning process, teachers develop a metacognitive understanding—a framework for learning about how and why learning occurs—in order to deepen the meaning of what is studied. If teachers and children understand the how and why, then they can reflect back on the learning as well as think forward, awakening more questions. Scheinfeld, Haigh, and Scheinfeld echo this idea: "Once the teachers started to listen, observe, reflect, and respond, the children's responses became focused and energized" (2008, 29). Early childhood education professionals can listen, observe, reflect, and respond while using mobile devices to enhance and streamline the documentation process.

Why technology matters

Technological documentation is a powerful tool for teachers as they plan and reflect in the moment on the curriculum. Gathering the digital records—photos, quotes, scanned work samples, commentary, and so forth—in a repository such as a password-protected blog or electronic journal helps teachers, families (including extended family and friends), and children make sense of and build on their own learning.

Classroom stories of teachers and technology

The following stories from our teacher research demonstrate the power of using technology in everyday classroom practices. We show how collaboration and group reflection help teachers make sense of technologically

Digital Documentation Tips

- Record the process (rather than product) of learning.
- Include the children's words.
- Add your own reflections.
- Document with children present and engaged with you in the documentation process.
- Ask the children about their process either while recording or when they're viewing the documentation later.
- Use questions that start with *what* or *how* (What were you thinking about when you chose to paint the flowers yellow? How did you make all the pieces fit in the box?).
- Have someone who can edit, get you to think more, and challenge you in positive ways review your documentation before you post it.
- Ask yourself what is most important—for example, the children's words, photographs of the children, or an artifact of the project. As you edit the presentation, check to see that what you value most is clearly visible, without distractions such as too many fonts, other visuals dominating and overlapping, or too many words. Consider leaving white space around the item.
- Keep the focus of the display on the children's ideas and work. For instance, use solid, muted colors; avoid borders; and use neutral colors for backgrounds. Children are natural designers; their work will provide the color and visual interest in the display.

By committing time and energy to documenting a child's work, teachers affirm that the child is a valued member of the learning community.

captured learning. We tell these stories in the first person to preserve their authenticity and keep our voices alive and coherent.

Reflections in the mirror (Jackie's story)

In a three-month study, I implemented new processes for documenting learning in my classroom of 3- to 5-year-olds. I introduced handheld video cameras and digital audio recorders to my two co-teachers, who began using the tools in their formal observations of the children. We reviewed the recordings in staff meetings to find patterns in the children's words and work—that is, recurring themes in class discussions. We took our discoveries back to the children to see how they responded to our ideas about their thinking.

While the children met in small groups, we also read back their words to them, played the videos, and showed them photographs. We asked the children to reflect on their learning experiences and activities as they looked through work artifacts, watched the videos, or listened to the recordings or transcriptions of their conversations. By the end of the study, we noticed changes in the way the children viewed their work and school.

At the beginning of the study, I asked the children what they learn at school. Their answers varied from "I don't know" to short lists of school activities. By the end of the study, the children's answers reflected their thinking about the process of learning: they gave reasons for why learning is necessary. Children identified examples of cognitive, social-emotional, and motor learning.

When I first asked Alice what she learns in school, Alice named sharing. At the end of the study, Alice gave not only a specific example of her learning, but also a theory for how she learned it:

Alice: I can do different things. I didn't climb on [the bars] at the park and a whole year went by when I didn't even try. I tried again, and I can do it. I didn't even practice, and then the next year I just tried again, and I could do it.

Jackie: How did that happen?

Alice: I think I just already knew how and then forgot.

Another child identified a social rule as something that she learned in school, and she explained why the rule exists: "[I learn] how to be nice and do things so the other people can treat you that way."

Bringing documentation of their words and learning back to the children seemed to add significance to them. As if looking in a mirror, the children watched themselves in the process of learning and saw themselves as powerful. What came through to the children as they watched the videos was my belief that their work is important. Because I value their work, the children themselves value their work.

Cat faces: Using a smartphone to learn more about children (Will's story)

In my role as a teacher researcher, I studied teachers' uses of technology in documentation with K–3 children at A Renaissance School of Arts and Sciences, where I am a board member. The school uses design technology (Dunn & Larson 1990) to engage children in active learning. In design technology, teachers and children collaborate to engineer and document projects that address a particular problem. The projects draw on children's creative, mathematical, scientific, engineering, technological, and/or expressive skills, knowledge, and ingenuity. Our problem centered on a small armature for a catlike creature. The armature, or basic structure, was made of rolled paper. It was covered in papier-mâché and wrapped in faux fur. The cat needed a face: eyes, nose, mouth, and whiskers.

I observed the children as they worked on pen-and-ink drawings to design a face for the creature. Using my smartphone, I snapped photographs of the children's drawings and sent them by e-mail to their teacher to talk about with the children. The teacher and I wanted to find out what the children were learning about cats as they drew the faces, and how they were researching the eyes, nose, mouth, and so forth, to draw. Meeting with children in small groups, the teacher talked with them about the photos and the questions. One child, age 6, said, "I saw that the creature needed a face, so I wanted to make sure it had whiskers. It seemed so lonely looking down at us without a face."

Using a smartphone, the children began a small research project on the facial features of cats. A 7-year-old shared his experience of searching the Internet and seeing how lions and domestic cats were similar and different: "Cats' pupils become vertical slits to filter light, while lions' don't; they are round, like ours." We (children and teachers together) put up our digital images on the school's blog and wrote down the children's stories on a tablet. We saved the digital stories as PDFs for easy uploading and future access. Parents commented on the project via the blog. Some parents shared how they too were learning about cats. One reported feeling closer to her child's learning through "reading and talking about the drawings on the blog" with her child.

Important General Tips

- Obtain written permission from the family before posting photos of their child on a website or in a blog.
- Be sure to include all children in videos and photos. Children will feel valued and families will know that their children are an important part of the learning community.

The smartphone and tablet proved critical as research and communication tools in this design technology experience. Without my phone handy, I might not have taken the initial photos, and the learning journey might have been lost to other events. The smartphone allowed the children to research and access relevant project data. We wonder if the children would have uncovered the richness in the data without having the Internet at their fingertips. Most important, the school blog allowed for family, teacher, and child interactions, permitting closeness to develop around the learning.

Limitations of handheld technology

Among the limitations we experienced in this teacher research project are negative attitudes toward mobile devices in the classroom, the time commitment for learning about the various technologies, staying present while using a technology tool, and keeping children focused on the learning and not on the technology to the exclusion of the learning.

In some settings, teachers are not allowed to use smartphones in their classrooms. This view of mobile devices may change as administrators see the potential uses for these devices beyond personal communication, and how they benefit the whole learning community. For these teachers, we recommend using touchscreen MP3 players, which have many of the same features as smartphones.

As for the learning curve with new technology, we learn as we practice. We search the web to watch basic technical or how-to videos that aid in our understanding and offer tips for using a tool. Web searches for these are becoming easier, and tips are often available from multiple users, from novices to experts, and in click-to-watch video format. Then we begin to learn in real time by using the technology tool on the job. Finally, we meet up with others to discuss what we have learned about the tech-

nology and what the documentation teaches us about children's learning and our teaching.

Operating a handheld technology device at first tends to take concentration. However, the more we are "behind the lens," the more the lens becomes part of our being present in the moment. This may be a matter of learning the language of technology, just as children learn the language of clay, paint, and drawing in "the hundred languages of children" (Edwards, Gandini, & Forman 1998).

The children's attitudes toward technology tools follow our attitudes. We engage the children naturally in our uses of technology in the classroom. The technology is merely a tool, and we learn about it alongside the children. The technology exists in the classroom for the sake of the learning, capturing the learning to make it visible and valued.

Another limitation of using mobile devices is the quality of the recordings. Though photography and display quality is improving, it still is not comparable to the quality of most cameras or monitors. However, in a fast-paced classroom, the devices' convenience and portability outweigh the drawbacks.

The technology is merely a tool, and we learn about it alongside the children.

Learning about technology

As we look back at our stories, we realize that technology has influenced our ability to retell learning experiences. We can look at a photo, video, blog, or website repeatedly to recall past events and share more of the details with families, children, and colleagues. This habit of looking back with children at their shared work and learning brings joy to the learning and our everyday experiences. Being open to the trends in technology and trying out multiple ways of recounting learning have made the documentation process integral to our work in understanding children's learning and development.

The reflections in the mirror and cat face stories show how teachers' technology skills and their ideas for using technology grow. Handheld devices help teachers maintain learning blogs and make them readily available

Mobile Technology Tips

- Keep your device with you and be ready to document.
- Upload media directly to a video-sharing website (such as YouTube or Vimeo) and your classroom blog.
- Keep blogs and websites secure by requiring users to enter a password.
- Keep notes in the notebook function or use an application like Evernote for mobile devices.
- Organize photos using web albums or photo-organizing software.
- If you have trouble operating your device, use a search engine such as Google or ask.com to search the Internet for help.

to families and to members of the internal school community who may be involved or want to learn more about the learning process.

Further, since adding the web-accessible component, many teachers no longer need to print out large volumes of information around photos and text. They can now print a few pictures that relate to current learning and store most photos on the tablet. With the tablet's larger screen, the photos and videos are big enough to be seen by all children at once. Limitations fall away as we continue to experiment.

Conclusion

Mobile devices and the documentation that they enable have the potential to change the way we assess students of all ages, expanding current testing practices into a more open-ended, child-driven, and sophisticated

method of assessing and communicating learning. However, to achieve this level of making learning visible, we need many more studies to corroborate the evidence presented here and elsewhere on the role of mobile technology in documenting children's learning.

As for our personal research, we plan to stay abreast of technological trends because, as technology makes our documentation work more efficient, we become freer to interact with young children, confident that we will have a record stored in the clouds for us to reflect on later.

References

Dunn, S., & R. Larson. 1990. *Design Technology: Children's Engineering.* London: The Falmer Press.

Edwards, C., L. Gandini, & G. Forman, eds. 1998. *The Hundred Languages of Children: The Reggio Emilia Approach—Advanced Reflections.* 2nd ed. Westport, CT: Ablex.

Malaguzzi, L. 1994. "Your Image of the Child: Where Teaching Begins." *Child Care Information Exchange* 96: 52–56. www.reggioalliance.org/downloads/malaguzzi:ccie:1994.pdf.

Malaguzzi, L. 1998. "History, Ideas and Basic Philosophy: An Interview with Lella Gandini." In Edwards, Gandini, & Forman, 49–97.

NAEYC & Fred Rogers Center for Early Learning and Children's Media at Saint Vincent College. 2012. "Technology and Interactive Media as Tools in Early Childhood Programs Serving Children from Birth through Age 8." Joint position statement. Washington, DC: NAEYC. www.naeyc.org/files/naeyc/file/positions/PS_technology_WEB2.pdf.

Project Zero & Reggio Children. 2001. *Making Learning Visible: Children as Individual and Group Learners.* Cambridge, MA: Project Zero.

Rinaldi, C. 2006. *In Dialogue with Reggio Emilia: Listening, Researching, and Learning.* New York: Routledge.

Scheinfeld, D.R., K.M. Haigh, & S.J.P. Scheinfeld. 2008. *We Are All Explorers: Learning and Teaching with Reggio Principles in Urban Settings.* New York: Teachers College Press.

Mobile Device Applications and Their Uses

App	Website	Description
BlogPress	blogpressapp.com	Allows you to type text and add photos and video from your mobile device to blog posts.
Blogger	blogger.com	Allows you to type text and add photos from your mobile device to a blog on Blogger.
Evernote	evernote.com	Lets you organize and store files, take notes, share specific folders with families, and use folders to maintain individual electronic portfolios for the children.
Quickoffice	quickoffice.com	Is similar to Microsoft Office Suite, but for mobile devices.
SoundNote	soundnote.com	Lets you type notes while recording audio. Later, selecting a word will play back the audio from the point that you typed that word. Great for documenting circle time discussions.

iDocument

How Smartphones and Tablets Are Changing Documentation in Preschool and Primary Classrooms

by Will Parnell and Jackie Bartlett

This article shares educators' experiences and strategies using mobile technology to document young children's learning.

Key messages

1. The purpose of documentation is to construct meaning from children's work. Meaning is built as the teacher and children reflect on their experiences.
2. Reflective documentation can shape children's self-images as learners. It provides the children with evidence that their work is important to the teacher and in the community.
3. Mobile technology can help early childhood educators with documentation, providing timely feedback to children and families by consolidating tools and data in one location.

In your view

1. What are the three most important themes or key ideas in this article? If possible, compare your choices with those of others who have read the article.
2. How is the content of this article related to applicable early learning standards or other curriculum or program requirements?

Reflect and revisit your practice

1. What ideas in this article affirm your practice? What questions does the article raise about your teaching practices? What new approaches might you try?
2. What kinds of supports do you and other teachers need to try out these new ideas?

Let's talk

1. What is your reaction to the teachers' use of mobile technology to document children's learning? How do you think you and the children you work with would benefit from using these strategies? What challenges might you face?
2. Take an inventory of the current digital and mobile technologies in your classroom. What do you need in order to digitally document learning on the Internet as described in the article?
3. As you work in digital documentation and blog publishing to make children's learning visible, how will you consider children's and adults' rights to privacy?
4. As you think about issues of equity and resources in your community, how can you communicate children's learning using technology with families who do not have access to the Internet? What resources might families need to engage with digital documentation?

Steps you can take

1. Develop procedures to keep mobile devices (or digital cameras) within easy reach as you work with children.
2. Implement your procedures by keeping your mobile device with you for several days as you work with children. Document the children's experiences that you want to share.
3. Share one of these experiences with the children's families through a blog or e-mail. Post a paper version for families without Internet access. Include your own thoughts about the video or photos. Why are you choosing this experience? How does it illustrate the children's development? How does it reflect their current interests? What does it say about the children or the environment?

Glossary

Documentation—a complex and ongoing process of capturing and making learning visible to invite children, educators, parents, and the surrounding community to interpret its meaning, which in turn shapes the image of the child and gives meaning to learning, teaching, and the purpose of school for young children.

Mobile technology—smartphones, tablets, and accompanying software and Internet blogs that can help teachers communicate important events in early childhood settings.

Teacher research—the process of actively listening, gathering, interpreting, and inquiring while being open to the child and to the encounters with and between children. The act of learning alongside of children and others.

To increase your knowledge

Project Zero & Reggio Children. 2001. *Making Learning Visible: Children as Individual and Group Learners.* Cambridge, MA: Project Zero.

Reggio Children. "The Wonder of Learning." www.thewonderoflearning.com/?lang=en_GB.

Scheinfeld, D.R., K.M. Haigh, & S.J.P. Scheinfeld. 2008. *We Are All Explorers: Learning and Teaching with Reggio Principles in Urban Settings.* New York: Teachers College Press.

Van Nood, R. Evernote as Portfolio. (blog) http://evernotefolios.wordpress.com.

Wheelock College. "Documentation: Transforming our Perspective." Video. Wheelock College Documentation Studio: Brookline, MA. http://vimeo.com/36323323.

Resources

Spotlight on Technology and Young Children

Young Children articles

An, H., & H. Seplocha. 2010. "Video-Sharing Websites: Tools for Developing Pattern Languages in Young Children." *Young Children* 65 (5): 20–25. www.naeyc.org/files/yc/file/201009/An Online0910.pdf.

Blagojevic, B., & K. Thomes. 2008. "Young Photographers: Can 4-Year-Olds Use a Digital Camera as a Tool for Learning? An Investigation in Progress . . ." *Young Children* 63 (5): 66–72.

Donohue, C., S. Fox, & D. Torrence. 2007. "Early Childhood Educators as eLearners: Engaging Approaches to Teaching and Learning Online." *Young Children* 62 (4): 34–40. www.naeyc.org/files/yc/file/200707/Donohue.pdf.

Kirchen, D.J. 2011. "Making and Taking Virtual Field Trips in Pre-K and the Primary Grades." *Young Children* 66 (6): 22–26.

Lisenbee, P. 2009. "Whiteboards and Web Sites: Digital Tools for the Early Childhood Curriculum." *Young Children* 64 (6): 92–95.

Technology and Young Children Interest Forum Members. 2008. "Meaningful Technology Integration in Early Learning Environments." On Our Minds. *Young Children* 63 (5): 48–50. www.naeyc.org/files/yc/file/200809/OnOurMinds.pdf.

Young, D., & L.M. Behounek. 2006. "Kindergartners Use PowerPoint to Lead Their Own Parent-Teacher Conferences." *Young Children* 61 (2): 24–26.

Recent research reports

Barron, B., L. Bofferding , G. Cayton-Hodges, C. Copple, L. Darling-Hammond, & M.H. Levine. 2011. "Take a Giant Step: A Blueprint for Teaching Children in a Digital Age." New York: The Joan Ganz Cooney Center at Sesame Workshop. www.joanganzcooneycenter.org/Reports-31.html.

Chiong, C., & C. Shuler. 2010. "Learning: Is There an App for That? Investigation of Young Children's Usage and Learning with Mobile Devices and Apps." New York: The Joan Ganz Cooney Center at Sesame Workshop. www.joanganzcooneycenter.org/upload_kits/learningapps_final_110410.pdf.

Common Sense Media. 2011. "Zero to Eight: Children's Media Use in America." Research study. www.commonsensemedia.org/research/zero-eight-childrens-media-use-america.

Gutnick, A.L., M. Robb, L. Takeuchi, & J. Kotler. 2011. "Always Connected: The New Digital Habits of Young Children." New York: The Joan Ganz Cooney Center at Sesame Workshop. www.joanganzcooneycenter.org/upload_kits/jgcc_always connected.pdf.

Takeuchi, L.M. 2011. "Families Matter: Designing Media for a Digital Age." New York: The Joan Ganz Cooney Center at Sesame Workshop. www.joanganzcooneycenter.org/upload_kits/jgcc_familiesmatter.pdf.

Wartella, E., R.L. Schomburg, A.R. Lauricella, M. Robb, & R. Flynn. 2010. "Technology in the Lives of Teachers and Classrooms: Survey of Classroom Teachers and Family Child Care Providers." Latrobe, PA: Fred Rogers Center for Early Learning and Children's Media at Saint Vincent College. www.fredrogers center.org/media/resources/TechInTheLivesofTeachers.pdf.

Other resources

Adams, M.J. 2011. "Technology for Developing Children's Language and Literacy: Bringing Speech-Recognition to the Classroom." New York: The Joan Ganz Cooney Center at Sesame Workshop. http://joanganzcooneycenter.org/Reports-30.html.

Bers, M.U. 2007. *Blocks to Robots: Learning with Technology in the Early Childhood Classroom.* New York: Teachers College Press.

Blanchard, J., & T. Moore. 2010. "The Digital World of Young Children: Impact on Emergent Literacy." Mill Valley, CA: Pearson Foundation. www.pearsonfoundation.org/literacy/research/emergent-literacy.html.

Borsheim, C., K. Merrit, & D. Reed. 2008. "Beyond Technology for Technology's Sake: Advancing Multiliteracies in the Twenty-First Century." *The Clearing House: A Journal of Education Strategies, Issues and Ideas* 82 (2): 87–90.

Brooks-Young, S.J., ed. 2010. *Teaching with the Tools Kids Really Use: Learning with Web and Mobile Technologies.* Thousand Oaks, CA: Corwin Press.

Couse, L.J., & D.W. Chen. 2010. "A Tablet Computer for Young Children? Exploring Its Viability for Early Childhood Education." *Journal of Research on Technology in Education* 43 (1): 75–98. http://eps415group4.pbworks.com/f/A%2520Tablet%2520 Computer%2520for%2520Young%2520Children.pdf.

Dell, A.G., D. Newton, & J. Petroff. 2011. *Assistive Technology in the Classroom: Enhancing the School Experiences of Students with Disabilities.* 2nd ed. Boston, MA: Allyn & Bacon.

Dolan, S., C. Donohue, L. Holstrom, L. Pernell, & A. Sachdev. 2009. "Supporting Online Learners: Blending High-Tech with High-Touch." *Exchange* 190: 90–97.

Edutopia. 2007. "What Is Successful Technology Integration? Well-Integrated Use of Technology Resources by Thoroughly Trained Teachers Makes Twenty-First-Century Learning Possible." www.edutopia.org/teaching-module-technology-integration-what.

Edutopia. 2011. "Home-to-School Connections Guide: Tips, Tech Tools, and Strategies for Improving Family-to-School Communication." www.edutopia.org/home-to-school-connections-guide.

Good, L. 2009. *Teaching and Learning with Digital Photography: Tips and Tools for Early Childhood Classrooms.* Thousand Oaks, CA: Corwin Press.

Jackson, S. 2011. "Spotlight: Quality Matters: Defining Developmentally Appropriate Media Use for Young Children." MacArthur Foundation (blog), March 16. Chicago, IL: MacArthur Foundation. http://spotlight.macfound.org/blog/entry/quality-matters-defining-developmentally-appropriate-media-use-for-young-ch.

Judge, S., K. Floyd, & T. Jeffs. 2008. "Using an Assistive Technology Toolkit to Promote Inclusion." *Early Childhood Education Journal* 36 (2): 121–26.

McPherson, S. 2009. "A Dance with the Butterflies: A Metamorphosis of Teaching and Learning through Technology." *Early Childhood Education Journal* 37 (3): 229–36.

Ntuli, E., & L. Kyei-Blankson. 2010. "Teachers' Understanding and Use of Developmentally Appropriate Computer Technology in Early Childhood Education." *Journal of Technology Integration in the Classroom* 2 (3): 23–35.

Puerling, B. 2012. *Teaching in the Digital Age: Smart Tools for Age 3 to Grade 3*. St. Paul, MN: Redleaf Press.

Rosen, D.B., & C. Jaruszewicz. 2009. "Developmentally Appropriate Technology Use and Early Childhood Teacher Education." *Journal of Early Childhood Teacher Education* 30 (2): 162–71.

Sadao, K.C., & N.B. Robinson. 2010. *Assistive Technology for Young Children: Creating Inclusive Learning Environments*. Baltimore, MD: Brookes.

Scheibe, C. & F. Rogow. 2012. *The Teacher's Guide to Media Literacy: Critical Thinking in a Multimedia World*. Thousand Oaks, CA: Corwin.

Serow, P., & R. Callingham. 2011. "Levels of Use of Interactive Whiteboard Technology in the Primary Mathematics Classroom." *Technology, Pedagogy, and Education* 20 (2): 161–73.

Simon, F., & C. Donohue. 2011. "Tools of Engagement: Status Report on Technology in Early Childhood Education." *Exchange* 199: 16–21.

Skouge, J.R., K. Rao, & P.C. Boisvert. 2007. "Promoting Early Literacy for Diverse Learners Using Audio and Video Technology." *Early Childhood Education Journal* 35 (1): 5–11.

Snider, S., & S. Hirschy. 2009. "A Self-Reflection Framework for Technology Use by Classroom Teachers of Young Learners." *He Kupu* 2 (1): 30–44. www.hekupu.ac.nz/Journal%20files/Issue1%20June%202009/A%20Self-Reflection%20Framework%20for%20Technology%20Use%20by%20Classroom%20Teachers%20of%20Young%20Learners.pdf.

Stephen, C., & L. Plowman. 2008. "Enhancing Learning with Information and Communication Technologies in Preschool." *Early Childhood Development and Care* 178 (6): 637–54. www.mendeley.com/research enhancing-learning- information-preschool.

US Department of Education. 2010. *Transforming American Education: Learning Powered by Technology. National Education Technology Plan 2010*. Washington, DC: Author. www.ed.gov/technology/netp-2010.

Wang, F., M.B. Kinzie, P. McGuire, & E. Pan. 2010. "Applying Technology to Inquiry-Based Learning in Early Childhood Education." *Early Childhood Education Journal* 37 (5): 381–89.

Young, S. 2009. "Towards Constructions of Musical Childhoods: Diversity and Digital Technologies." *Early Child Development and Care* 179 (6): 695–705.

Websites and online resources

Diigo Group—Blog, or follow others' postings and links to early childhood education technology articles. Join the group ECE-TECH, supported by NAEYC's Technology and Young Children Interest Forum, to archive pages, organize tagged items, and highlight sections of linked web pages or articles. You can also access your information via an iPhone app. **http://groups.diigo.com/group/ecetech**

Edutopia Elementary Tech Integration Blog—Elementary computer teacher Mary Beth Hertz writes this blog as part of the Edutopia website, offering her experiences and reflections about technology in early education. Updated approximately twice a month, recent posts discuss celebrating women and technology, educational apps in the classroom, and Internet research for elementary school children. **www.edutopia.org/blog/meaning-tech-integration-elementary-mary-beth-hertz**

Fred Rogers Center for Early Learning and Children's Media at Saint Vincent College—Available resources include issue briefings, an online support community, and a resource database of links to key organizations, publications, and media sources of early learning and children's media. The center also offers information on accessing the Fred Rogers archive, which includes Fred Rogers' speeches, his personal correspondence, and a digital audio and video archive from his television programs; and curriculum toolkits that provide assignments, in-class activities, syllabi, research links, and videos. **www.fredrogerscenter.org**

The center is also launching a new website, the **Fred Rogers Center Early Learning Environment**, or **Ele**, which offers free access to digital early learning resources, including an online community and library of 100+ free, high-quality e-books, mobile apps, and videos that support early learning and literacy. **www.ele.fredrogerscenter.org**

Hatch—Find links to industry research, ideas for obtaining grants, and free webinars on a variety of topics concerning different aspects of technology in early childhood education under the Research tab located at the top of the homepage. **www.hatchearlychildhood.com**

NAEYC—Read about and view NAEYC's recently updated technology joint position statement with the Fred Rogers Center. Find a brief summary of key messages from the statement and selected examples of effective classroom practice involving technology and interactive media. **www.naeyc.org/content/technology-and-young-children**

NAEYC Technology and Young Children Interest Forum—This NAEYC Interest Forum website is divided into sections: Technology with Children, Technology Tools for Educators, Technology at Home, and Research. Links include online activities, Internet safety, developmentally appropriate practice guidelines, apps, and web-based tools. The forum holds online discussions and meets yearly at NAEYC's annual conference. **www.techandyoungchildren.org/children.html**. The forum has also begun a wiki project where members can discuss early childhood education tech issues. **http://ecetech.wikispaces.com**

Technology in Early Childhood [TEC] Center at Erikson Institute—The TEC Center seeks to promote appropriate use of technology in early childhood settings. The site offers updated news and blog posts, upcoming center events, and offers a free webinar series, Early Childhood Investigations, taught by leaders in the field of education and technology. **www.teccenter.erikson.edu**

University of Maine Listserv—Follow and post current news about technology in early childhood education. The web archive interface is available for anyone to view. However, you must sign up and log in to post to the listserv. Subscribers can see and manage different lists. **www.lsoft.com/scripts/wl.exe?SL1=ECETECH-L&H=LISTS.Maine.Edu**

Technology and Interactive Media as Tools in Early Childhood Programs Serving Children from Birth through Age 8

A joint position statement of the National Association for the Education of Young Children and the Fred Rogers Center for Early Learning and Children's Media at Saint Vincent College

Television was once the newest technology in our homes, and then came videos and computers. Today's children are growing up in a rapidly changing digital age that is far different from that of their parents and grandparents. A variety of technologies are all around us in our homes, offices, and schools. When used wisely, technology and media can support learning and relationships. Enjoyable and engaging shared experiences that optimize the potential for children's learning and development can support children's relationships both with adults and their peers.

Thanks to a rich body of research, we know much about how young children grow, learn, play, and develop. There has never been a more important time to apply principles of development and learning when considering the use of cutting-edge technologies and new media. When the integration of technology and *interactive media* in early childhood programs is built upon solid developmental foundations, and early childhood professionals are aware of both the challenges and the opportunities, educators are positioned to improve program quality by intentionally leveraging the potential of technology and media for the benefit of every child.

This 2012 position statement reflects the ever-changing digital age and provides guidance for early childhood educators about the use of technology and interactive media in ways that can optimize opportunities for young children's cognitive, social, emotional, physical, and linguistic development. In this position statement, the definition of technology tools encompasses a broad range of digital devices such as computers,

Interactive media refers to digital and analog materials, including software programs, applications (apps), broadcast and streaming media, some children's television programming, e-books, the Internet, and other forms of content designed to facilitate active and creative use by young children and to encourage social engagement with other children and adults.

tablets, multitouch screens, interactive whiteboards, mobile devices, cameras, DVD and music players, audio recorders, electronic toys, games, e-book readers, and older analog devices still being used such as tape recorders, VCRs, VHS tapes, record and cassette players, light tables, projectors, and microscopes.

Throughout the process of researching and writing this position statement, we have been guided by the legacy of Fred Rogers. By appropriately and intentionally using the technology of his day—broadcast television—to connect with each individual child and with parents and families, Fred Rogers demonstrated the positive potential of using technology and media in ways that are grounded in principles of child development.

Statement of the Issues

Technology and interactive media are here to stay. Young children live in a world of interactive media. They are growing up at ease with digital devices that are rapidly becoming the tools of the culture at home, at school, at work, and in the community (Kerawalla & Crook 2002; Calvert et al. 2005; National Institute for Literacy 2008; Buckleitner 2009; Lisenbee 2009; Berson & Berson 2010; Chiong & Shuler 2010; Couse & Chen 2010; Rideout, Lauricella, & Wartella 2011). Technology tools for communication, collaboration, social networking, and user-generated content have transformed mainstream culture. In particular, these tools have transformed how parents and families manage their daily lives and seek out entertainment, how teachers use materials in the classroom with young children and communicate with parents and families, and how we deliver teacher education and professional development (Rideout, Vandewater, & Wartella 2003; Roberts & Foehr 2004; Rideout & Hamel 2006; Rideout 2007; Foundation for Excellence in Education 2010; Gutnick et al. 2010; Barron et al. 2011; Jackson 2011a, 2011b; Wahi et al. 2011). The pace of change is so rapid that society is experiencing a disruption almost as significant as when

FRED ROGERS CENTER
for early learning and children's media
at Saint Vincent College

The term *digital literacy* is used throughout this statement to encompass both technology and media literacy.

there was a shift from oral language to print literacy, and again when the printing press expanded access to books and the printed word. The shift to new media literacies and the need for *digital literacy* that encompasses both technology and media literacy will continue to shape the world in which young children are developing and learning (Linebarger & Piotrowski 2009; Flewitt 2011; Alper n.d.).

The prevalence of electronic media in the lives of young children means that they are spending an increasing number of hours per week in front of and engaged with screens of all kinds, including televisions, computers, smartphones, tablets, handheld game devices, and game consoles (Common Sense Media 2011). The distinction among the devices, the content, and the user experience has been blurred by multitouch screens and movement-activated technologies that detect and respond to the child's movements. With guidance, these various technology tools can be harnessed for learning and development; without guidance, usage can be inappropriate and/or interfere with learning and development.

There are concerns about whether young children should have access to technology and screen media in early childhood programs. Several professional and public health organizations and child advocacy groups concerned with child development and health issues such as obesity have recommended that passive, *non-interactive* technology and screen media not be used in early childhood programs and that there be no screen time for infants and toddlers. NAEYC and the Fred Rogers Center are also concerned about child development and child health issues and have considered them carefully when developing this position statement.

The American Academy of Pediatrics (2009, 2010, 2011a, 2011b) and the White House Task Force on Childhood Obesity (2010) discourage any amount or type of screen media and screen time for children under 2 years of age and recommend no more than one to two hours of total screen time per day for children older than 2 (Funk et al. 2009; Campaign for a Commercial-Free Childhood 2010). The Early Childhood Obesity Prevention Policies (Birch, Parker, & Burns 2011; Institute of Medicine of the National Academies 2011) recommend that child care settings limit screen time (including television, videos, digital media, video games, mobile media, cell phones, and the Internet) for preschoolers (age 2 through 5) to fewer than 30 minutes per day for children in half-day programs or less than one hour per day for those in full-day programs. The report further encourages professionals to work with parents to limit screen time to fewer than two hours per day for children age 2 through 5. These

recommendations to limit children's exposure to screen time are related to two factors potentially contributing to early childhood obesity: the food and beverage marketing that children may experience when they are watching television or interacting with other media and the amount of overall screen time to which they are exposed (Birch, Parker, & Burns 2011; Institute of Medicine of the National Academies 2011). The Let's Move! Child Care initiative recommends that caregivers allow no screen time for children under 2 years of age. For children 2 and older, caregivers are encouraged to limit screen time to no more than 30 minutes per week during child care, and parents and caregivers are advised to work together to limit children to one to two hours of quality screen time per day (Schepper 2011; White House 2011). Early childhood educators need to be aware of all these concerns and understand the critical role that they as educators play in mediating technology and media use and screen time for young children.

All screens are not created equal. The proliferation of digital devices with screens means that the precise meaning of "screen time" is elusive and no longer just a matter of how long a young child watches television, videos, or DVDs. Time spent in front of a television screen is just one aspect of how screen time needs to be understood and measured. Children and adults now have access to an ever-expanding selection of screens on computers, tablets, smartphones, handheld gaming devices, portable video players, digital cameras, video recorders, and more. Screen time is the total amount of time spent in front of any and all of these screens (Common Sense Media 2011; Guernsey 2011c). As digital technology has expanded in scope beyond linear, non-interactive media to include interactive options, it is evident that each unique screen demands its own criteria for best usage (Kleeman 2010). The challenge for early childhood educators is to make informed choices that maximize learning opportunities for children while managing screen time and mediating the potential for misuse and overuse of screen media, even as these devices offer new interfaces that increase their appeal and use to young children.

There is conflicting evidence on the value of technology in children's development. Educators and parents have been cautioned about the negative impact of background television (Kirkorian et al. 2009; AAP 2011b), passive use of screen media (AAP 2011b), and the relationship between media use and child obesity (White House Task Force on Childhood Obesity 2010; Birch, Parker, & Burns 2011; Schepper 2011). Possible negative outcomes have been identified, such as irregular sleep patterns, behavioral issues, focus and attention problems, decreased academic performance, negative impact on socialization and language development, and

Non-interactive media include certain television programs, videos, DVDs, and streaming media now available on a variety of screens. Non-interactive technology tools and media are not included in the definition and description of effective and appropriate use in this statement unless they are used in ways that promote active engagement and interactions. Non-interactive media can lead to passive viewing and overexposure to screen time for young children and are not substitutes for interactive and engaging uses of digital media or for interactions with adults and other children.

the increase in the amount of time young children are spending in front of screens (Cordes & Miller 2000; Appel & O'Gara 2001; Christakis et al. 2004; Anderson & Pempek 2005; Rogow 2007; Vandewater et al. 2007; Brooks-Gunn & Donahue 2008; Common Sense Media 2008, 2011; Lee, Bartolic, & Vandewater 2009; Campaign for a Commercial-Free Childhood 2010; DeLoache et al. 2010; Tomopoulos et al. 2010; AAP 2011a, 2011b).

However, research findings remain divided and therefore can be confusing to educators and parents. Some children's media researchers have found no evidence to support the belief that screen media are inherently harmful. The evidence from public broadcasting's Ready To Learn initiative suggests that when television shows and electronic resources have been carefully designed to incorporate what is known about effective reading instruction, they serve as positive and powerful tools for teaching and learning (Pasnik et al. 2007; Neuman, Newman, & Dwyer 2010; Corporation for Public Broadcasting 2011). Similarly, Wainwright and Linebarger (2006) concluded that while critics have issued many warnings against television and computers and their negative effects on children's learning, the most logical conclusion to be drawn from the existing scholarly literature is that it is the educational content that matters—not the format in which it is presented (Wainwright & Linebarger 2006). In short, there are some educationally valuable television shows, websites, and other digital media, and there are some that are less valuable or even educationally worthless.

The amount of time children spend with technology and media is important (Christakis & Garrison 2009; Vandewater & Lee 2009; Tandon et al. 2011), but how children spend time with technology must also be taken into account when determining what is effective and appropriate (Christakis & Garrison 2009; Tandon et al. 2011). The impact of technology is mediated by teachers' use of the same developmentally appropriate principles and practices that guide the use of print materials and all other learning tools and content for young children (Van Scoter, Ellis, & Railsback 2001; Clements & Sarama 2003a; Plowman & Stephen 2005, 2007).

The appeal of technology can lead to inappropriate uses in early childhood settings. Technology and media are tools that are effective only when used appropriately. The appeal of technology and the steady stream of new devices may lead some educators to use technology for technology's sake, rather than as a means to an end. Technology should not be used for activities that are not educationally sound, not developmentally appropriate, or not effective (electronic worksheets for preschoolers, for example). Passive use of technology and any type of screen media is an inappropriate replacement for active play, engagement with other children, and interactions with adults. Digitally literate educators who are grounded in child development theory and developmentally appropriate practices have the knowledge, skills, and experience to select and use technology tools and interactive media that suit the ages and developmental levels of the children in their care, and they know when and how to integrate technology into the program effectively. Educators who lack technology skills and digital literacy are at risk of making inappropriate choices and using technology with young children in ways that can negatively impact learning and development.

Issues of equity and access remain unresolved. The potential of technology and interactive media to positively influence healthy growth and development makes it important for early childhood educators to carefully consider issues of equity and access when they select, use, integrate, and evaluate technology and media. Early childhood educators have an opportunity to provide leadership in assuring equitable access to technology tools and interactive media experiences for the children, parents, and families in their care.

In the early 1960s, Head Start and other early childhood programs targeted the differences in access to print media for children from differing economic backgrounds. Today, educators face similar challenges with regard to technology tools, media, and broadband access to the Internet. Children growing up in affluent families more often have access to technology tools and broadband connections to the Internet in their homes, begin using the Internet at an early age, and have highly developed technology skills and beginning digital literacy when they enter school. Children in families with fewer resources may have little or no access to the latest technologies in their homes, early childhood settings, schools, or communities (Becker 2000; Burdette & Whitaker 2005; Calvert et al. 2005; National Institute for Literacy 2008; Cross, Woods, & Schweingruber 2009; Common Sense Media 2011).

Young children need opportunities to develop the early "technology-handling" skills associated with early digital literacy that are akin to the "book-handling" skills associated with early literacy development (National Institute for Literacy 2008). The International Society for Technology in Education (2007) recommends basic skills in technology operations and concepts by age 5. Early childhood settings can provide opportunities for exploring digital cameras, audio and video recorders, printers, and other technologies to children who otherwise might not have access to these tools. Educators should also consider the learning and creative advantage that high-quality interactive media can bring to children, especially when combined with skillful teaching and complementary curriculum resources that work together to accelerate learning and narrow the achievement gap between children from low-income families and their more affluent peers.

When educators appropriately integrate technology and interactive media into their classrooms, equity and access are addressed by providing opportunities for all children to participate and learn (Judge, Puckett, & Cabuk 2004; Cross, Woods, & Schweingruber 2009). In such an environment, accommodations are made for children with special needs to use technology independently (Hasselbring & Glaser 2000), and technology strategies to support dual language learners are in place.

Issues of equity and access also have implications for early childhood professionals and policy makers. Some early childhood educators face the same challenges in their own access to technology tools and Internet broadband at work or home as do the families of children in their care. Research and awareness of the value of technology tools and interactive media in early childhood education need to be shared with policy makers who are interested in issues of access and equity for children, parents, families, and teachers.

The Position

It is the position of NAEYC and the Fred Rogers Center that:

Technology and interactive media are tools that can promote effective learning and development when they are used intentionally by early childhood educators, within the framework of developmentally appropriate practice (NAEYC 2009a), to support learning goals established for individual children. The framework of developmentally appropriate practice begins with knowledge about what children of the age and developmental status represented in a particular group are typically like. This knowledge provides a general idea of the activities, routines, interactions, and curriculum that should be effective. Each child in the particular group is then considered both as an individual and within the context of that child's specific family, community, culture, linguistic norms, social group, past experience (including learning and behavior), and current circumstances (www.naeyc.org/dap/core; retrieved February 2, 2012).

Children's experiences with technology and interactive media are increasingly part of the context of their lives, which must be considered as part of the developmentally appropriate framework.

To make informed decisions regarding the intentional use of technology and interactive media in ways that support children's learning and development, early childhood teachers and staff need information and resources on the nature of these tools and the implications of their use with children.

NAEYC and the Fred Rogers Center offer the following principles to guide the use of technology and interactive media in early childhood programs.

Principles to Guide the Appropriate Use of Technology and Interactive Media as Tools in Early Childhood Programs Serving Children from Birth through Age 8

Above all, the use of technology tools and interactive media should not harm children. The healthy cognitive, social, emotional, physical, and linguistic development of the whole child is as important in the digital age as ever. Access to technology tools and interactive media should not exclude, diminish, or interfere with children's healthy communication, social interactions, play, and other developmentally appropriate activities with peers, family members, and teachers. Technology and media should never be used in ways that are *emotionally damaging, physically harmful, disrespectful, degrading, dangerous, exploitative,* or *intimidating to children.* This includes undue exposure to violence or highly sexualized images (NAEYC 1994; AAP 2009).

Just as early childhood educators always have been encouraged and advised to monitor and apply the latest research findings in areas such as health and child development, so too should they continually monitor and assess research findings on emerging issues related to technology,

including 3D vision and eye health, exposure to electromagnetic fields and radiation from cellular phones (EMR Policy Institute 2011), toxins from lead paint or batteries, choking hazards involving small parts, child obesity, screen time, or any other potentially harmful, physiological, or developmental effects or side effects related to the use of technology.

Developmentally appropriate practices must guide decisions about whether and when to integrate technology and interactive media into early childhood programs. Appropriate technology and media use balances and enhances the use of essential materials, activities, and interactions in the early childhood setting, becoming part of the daily routine (Anderson 2000; Van Scoter, Ellis, & Railsback 2001; Copple & Bredekamp 2009; NAEYC 2009a). Technology and media should not replace activities such as creative play, real-life exploration, physical activity, outdoor experiences, conversation, and social interactions that are important for children's development. Technology and media should be used to support learning, not an isolated activity, and to expand young children's access to new content (Guernsey 2010a, 2011b).

For infants and toddlers, responsive interactions between adults and children are essential to early brain development and to cognitive, social, emotional, physical, and linguistic development. NAEYC and the Fred Rogers Center join the public health community in discouraging the use of screen media for children under the age of 2 in early childhood programs. Recognizing that there may be appropriate uses of technology for infants and toddlers in some contexts (for example, viewing digital photos, participating in Skype interactions with loved ones, co-viewing e-books, and engaging with some interactive apps), educators should limit the amount of screen time and, as with all other experiences and activities with infants and toddlers, ensure that any use of technology and media serves as a way to strengthen adult-child relationships. Early childhood educators always should use their knowledge of child development and effective practices to carefully and intentionally select and use technology and media if and when it serves healthy development, learning, creativity, interactions with others, and relationships. This is especially true for those working with infants and toddlers.

Professional judgment is required to determine if and when a specific use of technology or media is age appropriate, individually appropriate, and culturally and linguistically appropriate. Early childhood educators are the decision makers in whether, how, what, when, and why technology and media are implemented through applying their expertise and knowledge of child development and learning, individual children's interests and readiness, and the social and cultural contexts in which children live. The adult's role is critical in making certain that thoughtful planning, careful implementation, reflection, and evaluation all guide decision making about how to introduce and integrate any form of technology or media into the classroom experience. Selecting appropriate technology and media for the classroom is similar to choosing any other learning material. Teachers must constantly make reflective, responsive, and intentional judgments to promote positive outcomes for each child (NAEYC 2009a).

Developmentally appropriate teaching practices must always guide the selection of any classroom materials, including technology and interactive media. Teachers must take the time to evaluate and select technology and media for the classroom, carefully observe children's use of the materials to identify opportunities and problems, and then make appropriate adaptations. They must be willing to learn about and become familiar with new technologies as they are introduced and be intentional in the choices they make, including ensuring that content is developmentally appropriate and that it communicates anti-bias messages.

When selecting technology and media for children, teachers should not depend on unverifiable claims included in a product's marketing material. In the selection process, program directors and teachers should consider the allocation of limited resources and cost effectiveness, including initial cost, the ongoing costs of updating and upgrading hardware and software, and other nonspecified costs such as additional items needed to use the product. Other considerations include durability for active use by young children and replacement costs if the device is dropped or damaged. Incentives for children to use the product or buy more products from the vendor should be reviewed and considered carefully. If developers and publishers of technology and media commit to using research-based information in the development, marketing, and promotion of their products, the selection of technology and interactive media tools will be less driven by commercial concerns and will become less mysterious and easier to choose for teachers and parents (Buckleitner 2011a; Fred Rogers Center n.d.).

Appropriate use of technology and media depends on the age, developmental level, needs, interests, linguistic background, and abilities of each child. There is a developmental progression in children's use of tools and materials, typically moving from exploration to mastery and then to functional subordination (using the tools to accomplish other tasks). Anecdotal evidence suggests this same progression is evident in the ways that children interact with technology tools. Children need time to explore the functionality of technology before they can be expected to use these tools to communicate. Just as we encourage children to use crayons and paper well before we expect them to write their names, it seems reasonable to provide access to technology tools for exploration and experimentation.

Certainly, most technology and media are inappropriate for children from birth to age 2 (at the time of this writing), and there has been no documented association between passive viewing of screen media and specific learning outcomes in infants and toddlers (Schmidt et al. 2009). Infants and toddlers need responsive interactions with adults. Yet mobile, multitouch screens and newer technologies have changed the way our youngest children interact with images, sounds, and ideas (Buckleitner 2011b). Infant caregivers must be sure that any exposure to technology and media is very limited; that it is used for exploration and includes shared joint attention and language-rich interactions; and that it does not reduce the opportunities for tuned-in and attentive interactions between the child and the caregiver. Preschoolers have varying levels of ability to control technology and media, but

with adult mediation they can demonstrate mastery of simple digital devices and are often seen using the tools as part of their pretend play. School-age children who are more proficient in using technology can harness these tools to communicate ideas and feelings, investigate the environment, and locate information. As devices and apps become more user-friendly, younger children are becoming increasingly proficient in using technological tools to accomplish a task—making a picture, playing a game, recording a story, taking a photo, making a book, or engaging in other age-appropriate learning activities. Technology tools and interactive media are one more source of exploration and mastery.

Effective uses of technology and media are active, hands-on, engaging, and empowering; give the child control; provide adaptive scaffolds to ease the accomplishment of tasks; and are used as one of many options to support children's learning. To align and integrate technology and media with other core experiences and opportunities, young children need tools that help them explore, create, problem solve, consider, think, listen and view critically, make decisions, observe, document, research, investigate ideas, demonstrate learning, take turns, and learn with and from one another.

Effective technology tools connect on-screen and off-screen activities with an emphasis on co-viewing and co-participation between adults and children and children and their peers (Takeuchi 2011). These tools have the potential to bring adults and children together for a shared experience, rather than keeping them apart. For example, a caregiver may choose to read a story in traditional print form, as an interactive e-book on an electronic device, or both. When experienced in the context of human interaction, these different types of engagements with media become very similar. Early book reading and other joint adult-child exploration can include co-viewing and co-media engagement. Growing concerns that television viewing and computer games are taking time away from physical activities and outdoor play can be offset by the use of technology and interactive media that encourage outdoor exploration and documentation of nature or that integrate physical activity and encourage children to get up and be mobile rather than sit passively in front of a screen.

Technology and media are just two of the many types of tools that can be used effectively and appropriately with young children in the classroom. As with many things, technology and media should be used in moderation and to enhance and be integrated into classroom experiences, not to replace essential activities, experiences, and materials.

When used appropriately, technology and media can enhance children's cognitive and social abilities. Technology and media offer opportunities to extend learning in early childhood settings in much the same way as other materials, such as blocks, manipulatives, art materials, play materials, books, and writing materials. Screen media can expose children to animals, objects, people, landscapes, activities, and places that they cannot experience in person. Technology can also help children save, document, revisit, and share their real-life experiences through images, stories, and sounds.

The active, appropriate use of technology and media can support and extend traditional materials in valuable ways. Research points to the positive effects of technology in children's learning and development, both cognitive and social (Haugland 1999, 2000; Freeman & Somerindyke 2001; Heft & Swaminathan 2002; Clements & Sarama 2003a, 2003b; Fischer & Gillespie 2003; Rideout, Vandewater, & Wartella 2003; Greenfield 2004; Kirkorian, Wartella, & Anderson 2008; Linebarger, Piotrowski, & Lapierre 2009; Adams 2011). Additional research is needed to confirm the positive outcomes of technology tools on children's language and vocabulary development, logical-mathematical understanding, problem-solving skills, self-regulation, and social skills development.

Interactions with technology and media should be playful and support creativity, exploration, pretend play, active play, and outdoor activities. Play is central to children's development and learning. Children's interactions with technology and media mirror their interactions with other play materials and include sensorimotor or practice play, make-believe play, and games with rules. Therefore, young children need opportunities to explore technology and interactive media in playful and creative ways. Appropriate experiences with technology and media allow children to control the medium and the outcome of the experience, to explore the functionality of these tools, and to pretend how they might be used in real life. Increasingly, educational media producers are exploring the learning power of interactive games and collaborative play involving children and their family members or teachers. Digital games fall into a similar category as board games and other self-correcting learning activities, with the same opportunities and cautions related to children's developmental stages.

Technology tools can help educators make and strengthen home–school connections. With technology becoming more prevalent as a means of sharing information and communicating with one another, early childhood educators have an opportunity to build stronger relationships with parents and enhance family engagement. Early childhood educators always have had a responsibility to support parents and families by sharing knowledge about child development and learning. Technology tools offer new opportunities for educators to build relationships, maintain ongoing communication, and exchange information and share online resources with parents and families. Likewise, parents and families can use technology to ask questions, seek advice, share information about their child, and feel more engaged in the program and their child's experiences there.

Technology tools such as smartphones, mobile devices, and apps offer new and more affordable ways for busy family members to communicate, connect to the Internet, and access information and social media tools to stay in touch with their families and their child's teachers and caregivers. Internet-based communication tools offer new opportunities for video calling and conferencing when face-to-face meetings are not possible; these same technology tools can connect children to other family members who live at a distance. As they do for young children, educators have a responsibility to parents and families to model appropriate, effective, and positive uses of technology, media, methods of communication, and social media that are safe, secure, healthy, acceptable, responsible, and ethical.

Technology tools can support the ways educators measure and record development, document growth, plan activities, and share information with parents, families, and communities. Teachers can use digital portfolios that include photographs as well as audio and video recordings to document, archive, and share a child's accomplishments and developmental progression with families in face-to-face conferences or through communication and social media tools. Displaying photos in the classroom of children's drawings or block buildings, along with narratives dictated by the children or explanations of why these types of play are important, can help families understand the critical role of play in early childhood development. Sending weekly, monthly, or even daily updates through social media or e-mail can help families feel more connected to their children and their activities away from home. Inviting children to take a picture of something they have done and helping them upload the photo to a file that can be e-mailed promote children's understanding of ways to communicate with others while also contributing to their learning more about the functions of reading and writing.

Most educators understand the value of writing down or recording notes that a child may want to give to parents. Using e-mail, educational texting, or other communication tools demonstrates the same concept about communication and helps to build digital literacy skills at the same time. If information is stored on a computer, the photos and notes can be printed and given to families who do not use technology to send or receive messages (Edutopia 2010).

Modeling the effective use of technology and interactive media for parent communication and family engagement also creates opportunities to help parents themselves become better informed, empowers them to make responsible choices about technology use and screen time at home, engages them as teachers who can extend classroom learning activities into the home, and encourages co-viewing, co-participation, and joint media engagement between parents and their children (Stevens & Penuel 2010; Takeuchi 2011).

Technology and media can enhance early childhood practice when integrated into the environment, curriculum, and daily routines. Successful integration of technology and media into early childhood programs involves the use of resources such as computers, digital cameras, software applications, and the Internet in daily classroom practices (Edutopia 2007; Technology and Young Children Interest Forum 2008; Hertz 2011). True integration occurs when the use of technology and media becomes routine and transparent—when the focus of a child or educator is on the activity or exploration itself and not on the technology or media being used. Technology integration has been successful when the use of technology and media supports the goals of educators and programs for children, provides children with digital tools for learning and communicating, and helps improve child outcomes (Edutopia 2007).

Careful evaluation and selection of materials are essential in early childhood settings. For example, one of the earliest and most familiar technologies in early childhood settings is Froebel's use of blocks. Montessori materials are another example of what we consider to be traditional early childhood supplies. Felt-tipped markers brought a new way for children to explore graphic representation that fell somewhere between paintbrushes and crayons.

As the lives of children, parents, families, and educators are infused with technology and media, early childhood classrooms can benefit from the possibilities of extending children's learning through judicious use of these tools. As part of the overall classroom plan, technology and interactive media should be used in ways that support existing classroom developmental and educational goals rather than in ways that distort or replace them. For example, drawing on a touch screen can add to children's graphic representational experiences; manipulating colorful acetate shapes on a light table allows children to explore color and shape. These opportunities should not replace paints, markers, crayons, and other graphic art materials but should provide additional options for self-expression.

With a focus on technology and interactive media as tools—not as ends in and of themselves—teachers can avoid the passive and potentially harmful use of non-interactive, linear screen media that is inappropriate in early childhood settings. Intentionality is key to developmentally appropriate use. One must consider whether the goals can be more easily achieved using traditional classroom materials or whether the use of particular technology and interactive media tools actually extends learning and development in ways not possible otherwise.

Exciting new resources in today's technology-rich world, such as 3D-rendered collaborative games and immersive world environments, represent the next frontier in digital learning for our youngest citizens, leaving it to talented educators and caring adults to determine how best to leverage each new technology as an opportunity for children's learning in ways that are developmentally appropriate. Careful evaluation and selection of materials is essential for the appropriate integration of technology and media in early childhood settings.

Assistive technology must be available as needed to provide equitable access for children with special needs. For children with special needs, technology has proven to have many potential benefits. Technology can be a tool to augment sensory input or reduce distractions. It can provide support for cognitive processing or enhancing memory and recall. The variety of adaptive and assistive technologies ranges from low-tech toys with simple switches to expansive high-tech systems capable of managing complex environments. When used thoughtfully, these technologies can empower young children, increasing their independence and supporting their inclusion in classes with their peers. With adapted materials, young children with disabilities can be included in activities in which they once would have been unable to participate. By using assistive technology, educators can increase the likelihood that children will have the ability to learn, move, communicate, and create.

Technology has supported inclusive practices in early childhood settings by providing adaptations that allow children with disabilities to participate more fully. Augmen-tative communication devices, switches, and other assistive devices have become staples in classrooms that serve children with special needs. Yet, with all of these enhanced capabilities, these technologies require thoughtful integration into the early childhood curriculum. Educators must match the technology to each child's unique needs, learning styles, and individual preferences (Behrmann 1998; Muligan 2003; Sadao & Robinson 2010). It is critically important that all early childhood teachers understand and are able to use any assistive technologies that are available to children with special needs in their classrooms and to extend similar or comparable technology and media-based opportunities to other children in their classrooms.

Technology tools can be effective for dual language learners by providing access to a family's home language and culture while supporting English language learning. Research has shown that access to information in the home language contributes to young children's progress both in their home language and in English (Espinosa 2008). Digital technologies allow teachers to find culturally and linguistically appropriate stories, games, music, and activities for every child when there may be no other way to obtain those resources (Uchikoshi 2006; Nemeth 2009). Because every child needs active practice in the four domains of language and literacy (speaking, listening, writing, and reading), technology resources should support active learning, conversation, exploration, and self-expression. Technology should be used as a tool to enhance language and literacy, but it should not be used to replace personal interactions. The role of language in developing self-esteem and social skills must also be considered in making technology plans for diverse classrooms.

Digital technologies can be used to support home languages by creating stories and activities when programs lack the funds to purchase them or when languages are hard to find. Technology can be used to explore the cultures and environments that each child has experienced, and it allows children to communicate with people in their different countries of origin. Technology may be needed to adapt existing materials; for example, by adding new languages to classroom labels, translating key words in books and games, or providing models for the writing area. With technology, adults and children can hear and practice accurate pronunciations so they can learn one another's languages. If teachers do not speak a child's language, they may use technology to record the child's speech for later translation and documentation of the child's progress. As linguistic and cultural diversity continues to increase, early childhood educators encounter a frequently changing array of languages. Appropriate, sensitive use of technology can provide the flexibility and responsiveness required to meet the needs of each new child and ensure equitable access for children who are dual language learners (Nemeth 2009).

Digital literacy is essential to guiding early childhood educators and parents in the selection, use, integration, and evaluation of technology and interactive media. Technology and media literacy are essential for the adults who work with young children. The prevalence of technology and media in the daily lives of young children and their families—in their learning and in their work—will continue to increase and expand in more ways than we can predict. Early childhood educators need to understand that technology and media-based materials can vary widely in quality, and they must be able to effectively identify products that help rather than hinder early learning (NAEYC 2009a).

For the adults who work with young children, digital literacy includes both knowledge and competence. Educators need the understanding, skills, and ability to use technology and interactive media to access information, communicate with other professionals, and participate in professional development to improve learning and prepare young children for a lifetime of technology use. Digital and media literacy for educators means that they have the knowledge and experience to think critically about the selection, analysis, use, and evaluation of technology and media for young children in order to evaluate their impact on learning and development. Digital and media literacy for children means having critical viewing, listening, and Web-browsing skills. Children learn to filter the messages they receive to make wise choices and gain skills in effectively using technology and technology- and media-based information (NAMLE 2007; Rogow & Scheibe 2007; ISTE 2008a, 2008b; Center for Media Literacy 2010; Hobbs 2010). These habits of inquiry transfer to all areas of the curriculum and to lifelong learning.

Using technology to support practice and enhance learning requires professional judgment about what is developmentally and culturally appropriate (Hobbs 2010). Early childhood educators who are informed, intentional, and reflective use technology and interactive media as additional tools for enriching the learning environment. They choose technology, technology-supported activities, and media that serve their teaching and learning goals and needs. They align their use of technology and media with curriculum goals, a child-centered and play-oriented approach, hands-on exploration, active meaning making, and relationship building (Technology and Young Children Interest Forum 2008). They ensure equitable access so that all children can participate. They use technology as a tool in child assessment, and they recognize the value of these tools for parent communication and family engagement. They model the use of technology and interactive media as professional resources to connect with colleagues and continue their own educational and professional development.

***Digital citizenship* is an important part of digital literacy for young children.** Digital citizenship in the context of early childhood programs refers to the need for adults to help children develop an emerging understanding of the use, misuse, and abuse of technology and the norms of appropriate, responsible, and ethical behaviors related to online rights, roles, identity, safety, security, and communication. Adults have a responsibility to protect and empower children—to protect them in a way that helps them develop the skills they need to ultimately protect themselves as they grow—and to help children learn to ask questions and think critically about the technologies and media they use. Adults have a responsibility to expose children to, and to model, developmentally appropriate and active uses of digital tools, media, and methods of communication and learning in safe, healthy, acceptable, responsible, and socially positive ways.

Young children need to develop knowledge of and experiences with technology and media as tools, to differentiate between appropriate and inappropriate uses, and to begin to understand the consequences of inappropriate uses. Issues of cyber safety—the need to protect and not share personal information on the Internet, and to have a trusted adult to turn to—are all aspects of a child's emerging digital citizenship that can begin with technology and media experiences in the early years. Children need to be protected by educators and parents against exploitation for commercial purposes. A child's image should never be used online without parental consent (ISTE 2007). Digital citizenship also includes developing judgment regarding appropriate use of digital media; children and adults need to be able to find and choose appropriate and valid sources, resources, tools, and applications for completing a task, seeking information, learning, and entertainment.

Early childhood educators need training, professional development opportunities, and examples of successful practice to develop the technology and media knowledge, skills, and experience needed to meet the expectations set forth in this statement. In recent years, smartphones, tablets, apps, game consoles and handheld game devices, streaming media, and social media have found their way into the personal and professional lives of early childhood educators; into early childhood programs serving young children, parents, and families; and into the homes of young children (Donohue 2010a, 2010b; Simon & Donohue 2011). Early childhood educators, parents, and families need guidance to make informed decisions about how to support learning through technology and interactive media, which technology and media tools are appropriate, when to integrate technology and media into an early childhood setting and at home, how to use these tools to enhance communication with parents and families, and how to support digital and media literacy for parents and children.

To realize the principles and recommendations of this statement, early childhood educators must be supported with quality preparation and professional development. Early childhood educators need available, affordable, and accessible professional development opportunities that include in-depth, hands-on technology training, ongoing support, and access to the latest technology tools and interactive media (Appel & O'Gara 2001; Guernsey 2010b, 2011a; Barron et al. 2011). Educators must be knowledgeable and prepared to make informed decisions about how and when to appropriately select, use, integrate, and evaluate technology and media to meet the cognitive, social, emotional, physical,

The term *digital citizenship* refers to the need for adults and children to be responsible digital citizens through an understanding of the use, abuse, and misuse of technology as well as the norms of appropriate, responsible, and ethical behaviors related to online rights, roles, identity, safety, security, and communication.

and linguistic needs of young children. Educators also need to be knowledgeable enough to answer parents' questions and steer children to technology and media experiences that have the potential to exert a positive influence on their development (Barron et al. 2011; Guernsey 2011b, 2011c; Takeuchi 2011).

Teaching in the age of digital learning also has implications for early childhood teacher educators in how they integrate technology tools and interactive media in the on-campus and online courses they teach, how well they prepare future early childhood teachers to use technology and media intentionally and appropriately in the classroom with young children and how well future teachers understand and embrace their role with parents and families (NAEYC 2009b; Rosen & Jaruszewicz 2009; Barron et al. 2011). Teacher educators need to provide technology-mediated and online learning experiences that are effective, engaging, and empowering and that lead to better outcomes for young children in the classroom. This requires knowledge of how adults learn and of how technology can be used effectively to teach teachers (NAEYC 2009b; Barron et al. 2011).

Current and future early childhood educators also need positive examples of how technology has been selected, used, integrated, and evaluated successfully in early childhood classrooms and programs. To implement the principles and recommended practices contained in this statement, educators need access to resources and online links, videos, and a professional community of practice in which promising examples and applications of emerging technologies and new media can be demonstrated, shared, and discussed.

Research is needed to better understand how young children use and learn with technology and interactive media and also to better understand any short- and long-term effects. The established body of research and literature on the effects of television viewing and screen time on young children, while foundational, does not adequately inform educators and parents about the effects of multiple digital devices, each with its own screen. As multitouch technologies and other emerging user interface possibilities become more affordable and available, new research is needed on what young children are able to do and how these tools and media can be integrated in a classroom. Research-based evidence about what constitutes quality technology and interactive media for young children is needed to guide policy and inform practice and to ensure that technology and media tools are used in effective, engaging, and appropriate ways in early childhood programs.

Recommendations

NAEYC and the Fred Rogers Center recommend that early childhood educators

1. Select, use, integrate, and evaluate technology and interactive media tools in intentional and developmentally appropriate ways, giving careful attention to the appropriateness and the quality of the content, the child's experience, and the opportunities for co-engagement.

2. Provide a balance of activities in programs for young children, recognizing that technology and interactive media can be valuable tools when used intentionally with children to extend and support active, hands-on, creative, and authentic engagement with those around them and with their world.

3. Prohibit the passive use of television, videos, DVDs, and other non-interactive technologies and media in early childhood programs for children younger than 2, and discourage passive and non-interactive uses with children ages 2 through 5.

4. Limit any use of technology and interactive media in programs for children younger than 2 to those that appropriately support responsive interactions between caregivers and children and that strengthen adult-child relationships.

5. Carefully consider the screen time recommendations from public health organizations for children from birth through age 5 when determining appropriate limits on technology and media use in early childhood settings. Screen time estimates should include time spent in front of a screen at the early childhood program and, with input from parents and families, at home and elsewhere.

6. Provide leadership in ensuring equitable access to technology and interactive media experiences for the children in their care and for parents and families.

Summary

This statement provides general guidance to educators on developmentally appropriate practices with technology and interactive media. It is the role and responsibility of the educator to make informed, intentional, and appropriate choices about if, how, and when technology and media are used in early childhood classrooms for children from birth through age 8. Technology and interactive media should not replace other beneficial educational activities such as creative play, outdoor experiences, and social interactions with peers and adults in early childhood settings. Educators should provide a balance of activities in programs for young children, and technology and media should be recognized as tools that are valuable when used intentionally with children to extend and support active, hands-on, creative, and authentic engagement with those around them and with their world.

Educators should use professional judgment in evaluating and using technology and media, just as they would with any other learning tool or experience, and they must emphasize active engagement rather than passive, non-interactive uses. To achieve balance in their programs and classrooms, they should weigh the costs of technology, media, and other learning materials against their program's resources, and they also should weigh the use of digital and electronic materials against the use of natural and traditional materials and objects.

Support for early childhood professionals is critically important. Educators need available, affordable, and accessible technology and media resources as well as access to research findings, online resources and links, and a professional community of practice. Preservice and professional development opportunities should include in-depth, hands-on technology experiences, ongoing support, and access to the latest technology tools and interactive media. To improve and enhance the use of technology and interactive media in early childhood programs, educators also need positive examples of how technology has been selected, used, integrated, and evaluated successfully in early childhood classrooms and programs.

Further research is needed to better understand how young children use and learn with technology and interactive media and also to better understand any short- and long-term effects. Research also is needed to support evidence-based practice for the effective and appropriate uses of technology and interactive media as tools for learning and development in early childhood settings.

References

AAP (American Academy of Pediatrics). 2009. "Policy Statement—Media Violence." *Pediatrics* 124 (5): 1495–503. www.pediatrics.org/cgi/doi/10.1542/peds.2009-2146.

AAP (American Academy of Pediatrics). 2010. "Policy Statement—Media Education." *Pediatrics* 126 (5): 1012–17. www.pediatrics.org/cgi/doi/10.1542/peds.2010-1636.

AAP (American Academy of Pediatrics). 2011a, June 13. Council on Communications and Media letter to the National Association for the Education of Young Children.

AAP (American Academy of Pediatrics). 2011b. "Policy Statement—Media Use by Children Younger Than 2 Years." *Pediatrics* 128 (5): 1–7. http://pediatrics.aappublications.org/content/early/2011/10/12/peds.2011-1753.

Adams, M.J. 2011. *Technology for Developing Children's Language and Literacy: Bringing Speech Recognition to the Classroom.* New York: The Joan Ganz Cooney Center at Sesame Workshop. http://joanganzcooneycenter.org/Reports-30.html.

Alper, M. "Developmentally Appropriate New Media Literacies: Supporting Cultural Competencies and Social Skills in Early Childhood Education." *Journal of Early Childhood Literacy* (forthcoming).

Anderson, D.R., & T.A. Pempek. 2005. "Television and Very Young Children." *American Behavioral Scientist* 48 (5): 505–22.

Anderson, G.T. 2000. "Computers in a Developmentally Appropriate Curriculum." *Young Children* 55 (2): 90–93.

Appel, A.E., & C. O'Gara. 2001. "Technology and Young Children: A Review of Literature." *TechKnowLogia* 3 (5): 35–36. http://ict.aed.org/infocenter/pdfs/technologyandyoung.pdf.

Barron, B., G. Cayton-Hodges, L. Bofferding, C. Copple, L. Darling-Hammond, & M.H. Levine. 2011. *Take a Giant Step: A Blueprint for Teaching Young Children in a Digital Age.* New York: Joan Ganz Cooney Center at Sesame Workshop. www.joanganzcooneycenter.org/Reports-31.html.

Becker, H.J. 2000. "Who's Wired and Who's Not: Children's Access to and Use of Computer Technology." *The Future of Children* 10 (2): 44–75. www.crito.uci.edu/tlc/FINDINGS/WhosWiredWhosNot.pdf.

Behrmann, M. 1998. *Assistive Technology for Young Children in Special Education: It Makes a Difference.* San Rafael, CA: The George Lucas Educational Foundation. www.edutopia.org/assistive-technology-young-children-special-education.

Berson, I.R., & M.J. Berson, eds. 2010. *High-Tech Tots: Childhood in a Digital World.* Charlotte, NC: Information Age Publishing.

Birch, L.L., L. Parker, & A. Burns, eds. 2011. *Early Childhood Obesity Prevention Policies.* Washington, DC: National Academies Press. www.iom.edu/Reports/2011/Early-Childhood-Obesity-Prevention-Policies.aspx.

Brooks-Gunn, J., & E.H. Donahue. 2008. "Introducing the Issue." *The Future of Children* 18 (1): 3–10. www.princeton.edu/futureofchildren/publications/docs/18_01_01.pdf.

Buckleitner, W. 2009. "What Should a Preschooler Know about Technology?" *Early Childhood Today.* www2.scholastic.com/browse/article.jsp?id=3751484.

Buckleitner, W. 2011a. *A Code of Ethics for the Publishers of Interactive Media for Children.* http://bit.ly/eo9cui.

Buckleitner, W. 2011b. "Setting Up a Multi-Touch Preschool." *Children's Technology Review* 19 (3): 5–9. www.childrenssoftware.com/pdf/g3.pdf.

Burdette, H.L., & R.C. Whitaker. 2005. "A National Study of Neighborhood Safety, Outdoor Play, Television Viewing, and Obesity in Preschool Children." *Pediatrics* 116 (3): 657–62. http://pediatrics.aappublications.org/content/116/3/657.full.

Calvert, S.L., V.J. Rideout, J.L. Woolard, R.F. Barr, & G.A. Strouse. 2005. "Age, Ethnicity, and Socioeconomic Patterns in Early Computer Use: A National Survey." *American Behavioral Scientist* 48 (5): 590–607.

Campaign for a Commercial-Free Childhood. 2010, July 26. CCFC letter to Jerlean Daniel, Executive Director, National Association for the Education of Young Children. www.commercialfreechildhood.org/pdf/naeycletter.pdf.

Center for Media Literacy. 2010. *MediaLit Kit.* Malibu, CA: Author. www.medialit.org/cml-medialit-kit.

Chiong, C., & C. Shuler. 2010. *Learning: Is There an App for That? Investigations of Young Children's Usage and Learning with Mobile Devices and Apps.* New York: The Joan Ganz Cooney Center at Sesame Workshop. http://pbskids.org/read/files/cooney_learning_apps.pdf.

Christakis, D.A., F.J. Zimmerman, D.L. DiGiuseppe, & C.A. McCarty. 2004. "Early Television Exposure and Subsequent Attentional Problems in Children." *Pediatrics* 113 (4): 708–13. http://pediatrics.aappublications.org/content/113/4/708.full.html.

Christakis, D.A., & M.M. Garrison. 2009. "Preschool-Aged Children's Television Viewing in Child Care Settings." *Pediatrics* 124 (6): 1627–32. http://pediatrics.aappublications.org/content/124/6/1627.full.

Clements, D.H., & J. Sarama. 2003a. "Strip Mining for Gold: Research and Policy in Educational Technology—A Response to 'Fool's Gold.'" *AACE Journal* 11 (1): 7–69.

Clements, D.H., & J. Sarama. 2003b. "Young Children and Technology: What Does the Research Say?" *Young Children* 58 (6): 34–40.

Common Sense Media. 2008. *Media + Child and Adolescent Health: A Systematic Review.* San Francisco: Author. http://ipsdweb.ipsd.org/uploads/IPPC/CSM%20Media%20Health%20Report.pdf.

Common Sense Media. 2011. *Zero to Eight: Children's Media Use in America.* San Francisco: Author. www.commonsensemedia.org/research/zero-eight-childrens-media-use-america.

Copple, C., & S. Bredekamp, eds. 2009. *Developmentally Appropriate Practice in Early Childhood Programs Serving Children from Birth through Age 8.* 3rd ed. Washington, DC: NAEYC.

Cordes, C., & E. Miller, eds. 2000. *Fool's Gold: A Critical Look at Computers in Childhood.* College Park, MD: Alliance for Childhood. http://drupal6.allianceforchildhood.org/fools_gold.

Corporation for Public Broadcasting. 2011. *Findings from Ready to Learn 2005–2010.* Washington, DC: Author. www.cpb.org/rtl/FindingsFromReadyToLearn2005-2010.pdf.

Couse, L.J., & D.W. Chen. 2010. "A Tablet Computer for Young Children? Exploring Its Viability for Early Childhood Education." *Journal of Research on Technology in Education* 43 (1): 75–98.

Cross, C.T., T.A. Woods, & H.A. Schweingruber, eds. 2009. *Mathematics Learning in Early Childhood: Paths toward Excellence and Equity.* Washington, DC: National Academies Press.

DeLoache, J.S., C. Chiong, K. Sherman, N. Islam, M. Vanderborght, G.L. Troseth, G.A. Strouse, & K. O'Doherty. 2010. "Do Babies Learn from Baby Media?" *Psychological Science* 21 (11): 1570–74. http://pss.sagepub.com/content/21/11/1570.

Donohue, C. 2010a. "There's an App for (Almost) Everything: New Technology Tools for EC Professionals—Part 2." *Exchange* 195: 40–44. https://secure.ccie.com/library/5019540.pdf.

Donohue, C. 2010b. "What's in Your Toolbox? New Technology Tools for EC Professionals—Part 1." *Exchange* 193: 82–87. https://secure.ccie.com/library/5019382.pdf.

Edutopia. 2007. *What Is Successful Technology Integration? Well-Integrated Use of Technology Resources by Thoroughly Trained Teachers*

Makes Twenty-First-Century Learning Possible. www.edutopia.org/technology-integration-guide-description.

Edutopia. 2011. *Home-to-School Connections Guide: Tips, Tech Tools, and Strategies for Improving Family-to-School Communication.* Rafael, CA: The George Lucas Educational Foundation. www.edutopia.org/home-to-school-connections-guide.

EMR Policy Institute. 2011, May 31. Letter to Jerlean Daniel, Executive Director, National Association for the Education of Young Children.

Espinosa, L.M. 2008. *Challenging Common Myths about Young English Language Learners.* FCD Policy Brief: Advancing PK–3, No. 8. New York: Foundation for Child Development. http://fcd-us.org/sites/default/files/MythsOfTeachingELLsEspinosa.pdf.

Fischer, M.A., & C.W. Gillespie. 2003. "Computers and Young Children's Development: One Head Start Classroom's Experience." *Young Children* 58 (4): 85–91.

Flewitt, R.S. 2011. "Bringing Ethnography to a Multimodal Investigation of Early Literacy in a Digital Age." *Qualitative Research* 11 (3): 293–310.

Foundation for Excellence in Education. 2010. *Digital Learning Now!* Tallahassee, FL: Author. www.excelined.org/Docs/Digital%20Learning%20Now%20Report%20FINAL.pdf.

Fred Rogers Center for Early Learning and Children's Media. *A Statement on the Development of a Framework for Quality Digital Media for Young Children.* Latrobe, PA: Fred Rogers Center for Early Learning and Children's Media at Saint Vincent College (forthcoming).

Freeman, N.K., & J. Somerindyke. 2001. "Social Play at the Computer: Preschoolers Scaffold and Support Peers' Computer Competence." *Information Technology in Childhood Education Annual* 1: 203–13.

Funk, J.B., J. Brouwer, K. Curtiss, & E. McBroom. 2009. "Parents of Preschoolers: Expert Media Recommendations and Ratings Knowledge, Media-Effects Beliefs, and Monitoring Practices." *Pediatrics* 123 (3): 981–88. http://pediatrics.aappublications.org/content/123/3/981.short.

Greenfield, P.M. 2004. "Developmental Considerations for Determining Appropriate Internet Use Guidelines for Children and Adolescents." *Applied Developmental Psychology* 25 (2004): 751–62. www.cdmc.ucla.edu/Published_Research_files/Developmental_considerations.pdf.

Guernsey, L. 2010a. "Screens, Kids, and the NAEYC Position Statement." *Early Ed Watch* (blog), August 2. Washington, DC: New America Foundation. http://earlyed.newamerica.net/blogposts/2010/screens_kids_and_the_naeyc_position_statement-35103.

Guernsey, L. 2010b. "When Young Children Use Technology." *Early Ed Watch* (blog), July 13. Washington, DC: New America Foundation. http://earlyed.newamerica.net/blogposts/2010/when_young_children_use_technology-34279.

Guernsey, L. 2011a. "EdTech for the Younger Ones? Not Without Trained Teachers." *Huffington Post* (blog), November 17. www.huffingtonpost.com/lisa-guernsey/edtech-for-the-playdough-_b_1097277.html.

Guernsey, L. 2011b. "A Modest Proposal for Digital Media in Early Childhood." *Early Ed Watch* (blog), June 24. Washington, DC: New America Foundation. http://earlyed.newamerica.net/blogposts/2011/a_modest_proposal_for_digital_media_in_early_childhood-53669

Guernsey, L. 2011c. "Young Kids and the Popularity of Digital 'Portability.'" *Early Ed Watch* (blog), March 24. Washington, DC: New America Foundation. http://earlyed.newamerica.net/blogposts/2011young_kids_and_the_popularity_of_digital_portability-47124.

Gutnick, A.L., M. Robb, L. Takeuchi, & J. Kotler. 2011. *Always Connected: The New Digital Media Habits of Young Children.* New York: The Joan Ganz Cooney Center at Sesame Workshop. http://joanganzcooneycenter.org/Reports-28.html.

Hasselbring, T.S., & C.H.W. Glaser. 2000. "Use of Computer Technology to Help Students with Special Needs." *The Future of Children* 10 (2): 102–22. http://familiestogetherinc.com/wp-content/uploads/2011/08/COMPUTERTECHNEEDS.pdf.

Haugland, S.W. 1999. "What Role Should Technology Play in Young Children's Learning? Part 1." *Young Children* 54 (6): 26–31.

Haugland, S.W. 2000. "What Role Should Technology Play in Young Children's Learning? Part 2." *Young Children* 55 (1): 12–18.

Heft, T.M., & S. Swaminathan. 2002. "The Effects of Computers on the Social Behavior of Preschoolers." *Journal of Research in Childhood Education* 16 (2): 162–74.

Hertz, M.B. 2011. "What Does 'Technology Integration' Mean?" *Edutopia* (blog), March 16. San Rafael, CA: The George Lucas Educational Foundation. www.edutopia.org/blog/meaning-tech-integration-elementary-mary-beth-hertz.

Hobbs, R. 2010. *Digital and Media Literacy: A Plan of Action.* Washington, DC: The Aspen Institute. www.knightcomm.org/wp-content/uploads/2010/12/Digital_and_Media_Literacy_A_Plan_of_Action.pdf.

Institute of Medicine of the National Academies. 2011. Early Childhood Obesity Prevention Policies: Goals, Recommendations, and Potential Actions. Washington, DC: Author. www.iom.edu/~/media/Files/Report%20Files/2011/Early-Childhood-Obesity-Prevention-Policies/Young%20Child%20Obesity%202011%20Recommendations.pdf.

ISTE (International Society for Technology in Education). 2007. *NETS for Students 2007 Profiles.* Washington, DC: Author. www.iste.org/standards/nets-for-students/nets-for-students-2007-profiles.aspx#PK-2.

ISTE (International Society for Technology in Education). 2008a. *The ISTE NETS and Performance Indicators for Teachers* (NETS-T). Washington, DC: Author. www.iste.org/Libraries/PDFs/NETS_for_Teachers_2008_EN.sflb.ashx.

ISTE (International Society for Technology in Education). 2008b. *NETS for Teachers.* 2nd ed. Washington, DC: Author. www.iste.org/standards/nets-for-teachers.aspx.

Jackson, S. 2011a. "Learning, Digital Media, and Creative Play in Early Childhood." *Spotlight on Digital Media and Learnng* (blog), March 24. Chicago, IL: MacArthur Foundation. http://spotlight.macfound.org/featured-stories/entry/learning-digital-media-and-creative-play-in-early-childhood.

Jackson, S. 2011b. "Quality Matters: Defining Developmentally Appropriate Media Use for Young Children." *Spotlight on Digital Media and Learning* (blog), March 16. Chicago, IL: MacArthur Foundation. http://spotlight.macfound.org/blog/entry/quality-matters-defining-developmentally-appropriate-media-use-for-young-ch.

Judge, S., K. Puckett, & B. Cabuk. 2004. "Digital Equity: New Findings from the Early Childhood Longitudinal Study." *Journal of Research on Technology in Education* 36 (4): 383–96. http://edinsanity.com/wp-content/uploads/2008/02/digital-equity_ecls.pdf.

Kerawalla, L., & C. Crook. 2002. "Children's Computer Use at Home and at School: Context and Continuity." *British Educational Research Journal* 28 (6): 751–71.

Kirkorian, H.L., E.A. Wartella, & D.R. Anderson. 2008. "Media and Young Children's Learning." *The Future of Children* 18 (1): 39–61. www.princeton.edu/futureofchildren/publications/docs/18_01_03.pdf.

Kirkorian, H.L, T.A. Pempek, L.A. Murphy, M.E. Schmidt, & D.R. Anderson, 2009. "The Impact of Background Television on Parent-Child Interaction." *Child Development* 80 (5): 1350–59.

Kleeman, D. 2010. "'A Screen Is a Screen Is a Screen' Is a Meme." *Huffington Post* (blog), December 8. www.huffingtonpost.com/david-kleeman/a-screen-is-a-screen-is-a_b_792742.html.

Lee, S-J., S. Bartolic, & E.A. Vandewater. 2009. "Predicting Children's Media Use in the USA: Differences in Cross-Sectional and Longitudinal Analysis." *British Journal of Developmental Psychology* 27 (1): 123–43.

Linebarger, D.L., & J.T. Piotrowski. 2009. "TV as Storyteller: How Exposure to Television Narratives Impacts At-Risk Preschoolers' Story Knowledge and Narrative Skills." *British Journal of Developmental Psychology* 27 (1): 47–69.

Linebarger, D.L., J.T. Piotrowski, & M. Lapierre. 2009. "The Relationship between Media Use and the Language and Literacy Skills of Young Children: Results from a National Parent Survey." Paper presented at the NAEYC Annual Conference, 18–21 November, Washington, DC.

Lisenbee, P. 2009. "Whiteboards and Websites: Digital Tools for the Early Childhood Curriculum." *Young Children* 64 (6): 92–95.

Muligan, S.A. 2003. "Assistive Technology: Supporting the Participation of Children with Disabilities." *Young Children* 58 (6): 50–51. www.naeyc.org/files/yc/file/200311/AssistiveTechnology.pdf.

NAEYC. 1994. "Media Violence in Children's Lives." Position statement. Washington, DC: Author. www.naeyc.org/files/naeyc/file/positions/PSMEVI98.PDF.

NAEYC. 2009a. "Developmentally Appropriate Practice in Early Childhood Programs Serving Children from Birth through Age 8." Position statement. Washington, DC: Author. www.naeyc.org/files/naeyc/file/positions/position%20statement%20Web.pdf.

NAEYC. 2009b. "NAEYC Standards for Early Childhood Professional Preparation Programs." Position statement. Washington, DC: Author. www.naeyc.org/files/naeyc/file/positions/ProfPrepStandards09.pdf.

NAMLE (National Association for Media Literacy Education). 2007. *Core Principles of Media Literacy Education in the United States.* http://namle.net/wp-content/uploads/2009/09/NAMLE-CPMLE-w-questions2.pdf.

National Institute for Literacy. 2008. *Developing Early Literacy: Report of the National Early Literacy Panel. A Scientific Synthesis of Early Literacy Development and Implications for Intervention.* T. Shanahan, Chair. Louisville, KY: National Center for Family Literacy.

Nemeth, K.N. 2009. *Many Languages, One Classroom: Teaching Dual and English Language Learners.* Silver Spring, MD: Gryphon House.

Neuman, S.B., E.H. Newman, & J. Dwyer. 2010. *Educational Effects of an Embedded Multimedia Vocabulary Intervention for Economically Disadvantaged Pre-K Children: A Randomized Trial.* Ann Arbor, MI: University of Michigan. www.umich.edu/~rdytolrn/pdf/RTL2021210.pdf.

Pasnik, S., S. Strother, J. Schindel, W.R. Penuel, & C. Llorente. 2007. *Report to the Ready To Learn Initiative: Review of Research on Media and Young Children's Literacy.* New York; Menlo Park, CA: Education Development Center; SRI International. http://ctl.sri.com/publications/downloads/EDC_SRI_Literature_Review.pdf.

Plowman, L., & C. Stephen. 2005. "Children, Play, and Computers in Pre-school Education." *British Journal of Educational Technology* 36 (2): 145–57.

Plowman, L., & C. Stephen. 2007. "Guided Interaction in Pre-school Settings." *Journal of Computer Assisted Learning* 23 (1): 14–26.

Rideout, V.J. 2007. *Parents, Children, and Media: A Kaiser Family Foundation Survey.* Menlo Park, CA: The Henry J. Kaiser Family Foundation. www.kff.org/entmedia/upload/7638.pdf.

Rideout, V.J., & E. Hamel. 2006. T*he Media Family: Electronic Media in the Lives of Infants, Toddlers, Preschoolers, and Their Parents.* Menlo Park, California: The Henry J. Kaiser Family Foundation. www.kff.org/entmedia/upload/7500.pdf.

Rideout, V.J., A. Lauricella, & E. Wartella. 2011. *Children, Media, and Race: Media Use among White, Black, Hispanic, and Asian American Children.* Evanston, IL: Center on Media and Human Development, School of Communication, Northwestern University. http://web5.soc.northwestern.edu/cmhd/wp-content/uploads/2011/06/SOCconfReportSingleFinal-1.pdf.

Rideout, V.J., E.A. Vandewater, & E.A. Wartella. 2003. *Zero to Six: Electronic Media in the Lives of Infants, Toddlers, and Preschoolers.* The Henry J. Kaiser Family Foundation. www.kff.org/entmedia/upload/Zero-to-Six-Electronic-Media-in-the-Lives-of-Infants-Toddlers-and-Preschoolers-PDF.pdf.

Roberts, D.F., & U.G. Foehr. 2004. *Kids and Media in America.* Cambridge, MA: Cambridge University Press.

Rogow, F. 2007. *Two View or Not Two View: A Review of the Research Literature on the Advisability of Television Viewing for Infants and Toddlers.* Ithaca, NY: Insighters Educational Consulting. www.kqed.org/assets/pdf/education/earlylearning/media-symposium/tv-under-two-rogow.pdf?trackurl=true.

Rogow, F., & C. Scheibe. 2007. *Key Questions to Ask When Analyzing Media Messages.* http://namle.net/wp-content/uploads/2009/09/NAMLEKeyQuestions0708.pdf.

Rosen, D.B., & C. Jaruszewicz. 2009. "Developmentally Appropriate Technology Use and Early Childhood Teacher Education." *Journal of Early Childhood Teacher Education* 30 (2): 162–71.

Sadao, K.C., & N.B. Robinson. 2010. *Assistive Technology for Young Children: Creating Inclusive Learning Environments.* Baltimore, MD: Brookes.

Schepper, R. 2011. "Introducing Let's Move! Child Care: Tools for Child and Day Care Centers and Family-Care Homes." *Let's Move* (blog), June 8. www.letsmove.gov/blog/2011/06/08/introducing-let%E2%80%99s-move-child-care-tools-child-and-day-care-centers-and-family-care-h.

Schmidt, M.E., M. Rich, S.L. Rifas-Shiman, E. Oken, & E.M. Taveras. 2009. "Television Viewing in Infancy and Child Cognition at 3 Years of Age in a U.S. Cohort." *Pediatrics* 123 (3): e370–e375. http://pediatrics.aappublications.org/content/123/3/e370.full.

Simon, F., & C. Donohue. 2011. "Tools of Engagement: Status Report on Technology in Early Childhood Education." *Exchange* 199: 16–22.

Stevens, R., & W.R. Penuel. 2010. "Studying and Fostering Learning through Joint Media Engagement." Paper presented at the Principal Investigators Meeting of the National Science Foundation's Science of Learning Centers, October, Arlington, VA.

Takeuchi, L.M. 2011. *Families Matter: Designing Media for a Digital Age.* New York: The Joan Ganz Cooney Center at Sesame Workshop. http://joanganzcooneycenter.org/Reports-29.html.

Tandon, P.S., C. Zhou, P. Lozano, & D.A. Christakis. 2011. "Preschoolers' Total Daily Screen Time at Home and by Type of Child Care." *Journal of Pediatrics* 158 (2): 297–300.

Technology and Young Children Interest Forum. 2008. "On Our Minds: Meaningful Technology Integration in Early Learning Environments." *Young Children* 63 (5): 48–50. www.naeyc.org/files/yc/file/200809/OnOurMinds.pdf.

Tomopoulos, S., B.P. Dreyer, S. Berkule, A.H. Fierman, C. Brockmeyer, & A.L. Mendelsohn. 2010. "Infant Media Exposure and Toddler Development." *Archives of Pediatrics & Adolescent Medicine* 164 (12): 1105–11. http://archpedi.ama-assn.org/cgi/content/full/164/12/1105.

Uchikoshi, Y. 2006. "Early Reading in Bilingual Kindergartners: Can Educational Television Help?" *Scientific Studies of Reading* 10 (1): 89–120.

Vandewater, E.A., & S-J. Lee. 2009. "Measuring Children's Media Use in the Digital Age: Issues and Challenges." *American Behavioral Scientist* 52 (8): 1152–76. www.ncbi.nlm.nih.gov/pmc/articles/PMC2745155/pdf/nihms128628.pdf.

Vandewater, E.A., V.J. Rideout, E.A. Wartella, X. Huang, J.H. Lee, & M. Shim. 2007. "Digital Childhood: Electronic Media and Technology Use among Infants, Toddlers, and Preschoolers." *Pediatrics* 119 (5): e1006-e1015. http://pediatrics.aappublications.org/cgi/content/full/119/5/e1006.

Van Scoter, J., D. Ellis, & J. Railsback. 2001. *Technology in Early Childhood Education: Finding the Balance.* Portland, OR: Northwest Regional Educational Laboratory. www.netc.org/earlyconnections/byrequest.pdf

Wahi, G., P.C. Parkin, J. Beyene, E.M. Uleryk, & C.S. Birken. 2011. "Effectiveness of Interventions Aimed at Reducing Screen Time in Children." *Archives of Pediatrics & Adolescent Medicine* 165 (11): 979–86.

Wainwright, D.K., & D.L. Linebarger. 2006. *Ready To Learn: Literature Review. Part 1: Elements of Effective Educational TV.* Philadelphia, PA: Annenberg School for Communication, University of Pennsylvania; American Institutes for Research. http://pbskids.org/read/files/BOB-PARTI-ElementsofSuccessfulEdTV.PDF.

White House Task Force on Childhood Obesity. 2010. *Solving the Problem of Childhood Obesity within a Generation.* Washington, DC: Office of the President of the United States. www.letsmove.gov/sites/letsmove.gov/files/TaskForce_on_Childhood_Obesity_May2010_FullReport.pdf.

White House. 2011. "First Lady Unveils Let's Move! Child Care to Ensure Healthy Start for Youngest Children," press release, June 8. Washington, DC: Office of the First Lady. www.whitehouse.gov/the-press-office/2011/06/08/first-lady-unveils-lets-move-child-care-ensure-healthy-start-youngest-ch.

Acknowledgments

NAEYC and the Fred Rogers Center (FRC) appreciate the work of the Joint NAEYC-FRC Writing Team and Working Group members who participated in the development of this position statement: Roberta Schomburg, Co-chair, Carlow University and Fred Rogers Center; Chip Donohue, Co-chair, Erikson Institute and Fred Rogers Center; Madhavi Parikh, NAEYC; Warren Buckleitner, Children's Technology Review; Pamela Johnson, Corporation for Public Broadcasting; Lynn Nolan, International Society for Technology in Education; Christine Wang, State University at Buffalo, SUNY; Ellen Wartella, Northwestern University and Fred Rogers Center. Input from members of the NAEYC Governing Board and the Fred Rogers Center Advisory Council, as well as key staff members in both organizations, also is acknowledged.